CW01666442

12

Der fliegende Holländer

The Flying Dutchman

Wagner

The first appearance of the Dutchman (Norman Bailey) in the 1982 ENO production, designed by Stefanos Lazaridis. (photo: Reg Wilson)

Preface

This series, published under the auspices of English National Opera and The Royal Opera, aims to prepare audiences to enjoy and evaluate opera performances. Each book contains the complete text, set out in the original language together with a current performing translation. The accompanying essays have been commissioned as general introductions to aspects of interest in each work. As many illustrations and musical examples as possible have been included because the sound and spectacle of opera are clearly central to any sympathetic appreciation of it. We hope that, as ideal companions to the opera should be, they are well-informed, witty and attractive.

Nicholas John
Series Editor

12

Der fliegende Holländer
The Flying Dutchman

Richard Wagner

Opera Guide Series Editor: Nicholas John

Published in association with English National Opera and The Royal Opera

John Calder · London
Riverrun Press · New York

First published in Great Britain, 1982, by
John Calder (Publishers) Ltd, 18 Brewer Street,
London W1R 4AS

and

First published in U.S.A., 1982, by
Riverrun Press Inc.,
175 Fifth Avenue,
New York, NY 10010

BRITISH LIBRARY CATALOGUING DATA
Wagner, Richard
Die fliegende Holländer — (English National Opera guide; 12)
1. Wagner, Richard. Fliegender Holländer
2. Operas — Librettos
I. Title II. John, Nicholas
III. Series
782.1'092'4 ML410.W14
ISBN 0 7145 3920 1

SUBSIDISED BY THE Arts Council OF GREAT BRITAIN

John Calder (Publishers) Ltd, English National Opera and The Royal Opera House, Covent Garden Ltd receive financial assistance from the Arts Council of Great Britain. English National Opera also receives financial assistance from the Greater London Council.

Typeset in Plantin by Margaret Spooner Typesetting
Printed and bound in Great Britain by Collins, Glasgow.

Contents

List of Illustrations vi

Behind 'The Flying Dutchman' *John Warrack* 7

An introduction to 'The Flying Dutchman' *John Deathridge* 13

Loneliness, Love and Death *William Vaughan* 27

The Overture to 'The Flying Dutchman' *Richard Wagner* 35

Remarks on Performing 'The Flying Dutchman' *Richard Wagner* 37

Thematic Guide 43

'Der fliegende Holländer' / 'The Flying Dutchman' 49
Poem by Richard Wagner
English translation by David Pountney

Act One 50

Act Two 58

Act Three 70

Discography 78

Bibliography 80

List of Illustrations

Cover:	Design by Kevin Scally.
Frontispiece:	The 1982 ENO production. (photo: Reg Wilson)
p. 8	Anton Van Rooy as the Dutchman. (Stuart-Liff Collection)
p. 8	Friedrich Plaschke as the Dutchman. (Royal College of Music)
p. 9	Carl Perron as the Dutchman. (Stuart-Liff Collection)
p. 9	Emmy Destinn as Senta. (Stuart-Liff Collection)
p. 10	Karl Scheidermantel as the Dutchman. (Royal College of Music)
p. 10	Johannes Bischoff as the Dutchman. (Stuart-Liff Collection)
p. 12	Friedrich Schorr as the Dutchman.
p. 12	Kirsten Flagstad as Senta.
p. 17	An unidentified early set for the first act. (Royal College of Music)
p. 18	The 1966 Covent Garden production. (photo: Donald Southern)
p. 19	Norman Bailey and Gwyneth Jones. (BBC Copyright photographs)
p. 20	Hans Hotter as the Dutchman. (Met. Archives)
p. 20	Viorica Ursuleac as Senta. (Ida Cook Collection)
p. 21	Ernestine Schumann-Heink as Mary. (Met. Archives)
p. 21	Annie Krull as Senta (Royal College of Music)
p. 22	Leonie Rysanek as Senta. (Stuart-Liff Collection)
p. 22	Set Svanholm as Erik at the Met. (Met. Archives)
p. 23	The 1982 ENO production. (photo: Reg Wilson)
p. 24	Eva van der Osten as Senta. (Stuart-Liff Collection)
p. 26	Otakar Kraus as the Dutchman.
p. 29	Design by Emil Preetorius. (Bayreuther Festspiele)
p. 30	'The Stages of Life' by Caspar David Friedrich.
p. 31	Barbara Kemp as Senta. (Stuart-Liff Collection)
p. 33	An unidentified early set. (Royal College of Music)
p. 33	Maurice Renaud as the Dutchman. (Stuart-Liff Collection)
p. 34	Donald McIntyre and Rita Hunter. (photo: Donald Southern)
p. 34	Norman Bailey and Harold Blackburn. (photo: Donald Southern)
p. 36	Harry Kupfer's Bayreuth production. (Festpielleitung Bayreuth)
p. 39	Heinrich Knöte as Erik in 1908. (Covent Garden Archives)
p. 41	The first Bayreuth cast — 1901. (Royal College ofMusic)
p. 48	*above* The 1982 ENO production. (photo: Reg Wilson) *below* The Opera North production. (photo: Robin Don)
p. 57	David Ward as the Dutchman. (photo: Reg Wilson)
p. 57	Herbert Jansen as the Dutchman. (Met. Archives)
p. 69	Dennis Wicks and Josephine Barstow. (photo: Reg Wilson)
p. 77	Everding's Bayreuth production. (Festspielleitung Bayreuth)

Behind 'The Flying Dutchman'

John Warrack

Wagner was fortunate to grow up in Dresden. As a child there, from 1814 to 1828, he overlapped with the period of Carl Maria von Weber's intendancy; his stepfather Ludwig Geyer was an actor and buffo tenor in the German company, his sisters sang in *Preciosa* and (later in Leipzig) in *Silvana*, and he himself as a child appeared in one of Weber's occasional pieces dressed up as an angel with wings sewn onto his back. He had already been spellbound by the figure of the frail Weber limping off to rehearsals, associating physical disability and the creative spark in his mind; and, he later wrote, '*Der Freischütz* in particular appealed to my imagination, mainly on account of its ghostly theme'. Among his earliest influences were two of the strains that were to meet in the work that was to give German Romantic opera new maturity, *The Flying Dutchman* – a lure towards the supernatural, and a wide knowledge of the operas that, especially in the repertory of Weber's German company in Dresden, were a creative basis for German Romantic opera.

Wagner seems never completely to have lost the enjoyment of the supernatural that was a fashion in his youth. Having absorbed the atmosphere of the novels of the so-called *Schauerromantik*, or Horror Romanticism, he wrote as his first creative effort a drama, *Leubald*, which he described with ironic amusement in his autobiography as an absurd farrago of Shakespeare and Goethe, thronged with menacing ghosts. 'The spirit world had a very real meaning for me', he wrote; and this was in connexion with a sound that was to haunt him all his life, the fifths on the open strings of an orchestra tuning up. Whatever the reason, it seized his imagination as 'a greeting from the spirit world'; the tremolo fifths opening Beethoven's Ninth Symphony sent shudders down his spine, and he was to reproduce them (he copied the whole score of the Ninth, and made a piano reduction) as the opening of his own youthful C major Symphony. This was hardly more than direct aural stimulus; that Wagner had also absorbed the dramatic import of the sound, as it struck his imagination, is shown at the beginning of the *Flying Dutchman* overture, where the barren fifths, neither major nor minor even in the horn call that storms through them, suggest a realm beyond such human definitions.

Wagner's absorption in the world of the supernatural was to take manifold forms. Like all his generation, he thrilled to the stories of E.T.A. Hoffmann. 'Now came the time when I really lived and breathed in Hoffmann's artistic atmosphere of ghosts and spirits', he recalled of his childhood years in his autobiography *Mein Leben*; a tale that particularly impressed him as a boy was *Der Magnetiseur*, Hoffmann's tale of a mesmerist. Together with the readings of Shakespeare, Calderón, Goethe and other great masters that occupied the evenings at Wahnfried, a place was regularly found for ghost stories; and though concerned not to frighten Cosima, he once badly upset her with his vivid reading of the ghost story *Das Majorat*. His projected first opera, *Die Hochzeit*, was sketched under the influence of Hoffmann, as he admitted; and he first came to know the story of the song contest on the Wartburg, part of the *Tannhäuser* plot, from Hoffmann's treatment of it. He was also, as a young man in Vienna, to take delight in the comedies of Ferdinand Raimund, whose inordinately popular pieces dealt often with the humour of transferring a plain Viennese citizen to the world of spirits,

Anton Van Rooy, the Dutch baritone, as the Dutchman. (Stuart-Liff Collection)

Friedrich Plaschke as the Dutchman. (Royal College of Music)

usually for the correction of his faults. Wagner praised Raimund's work in an essay, *Über Schauspieler und Sänger*; and a diary entry by Cosima, following a reading of Raimund, gives as the Wahnfried view that within the bounds of the Viennese popular theatre he was 'an incomparable genius'. There is a line to be traced from these amiable plays, tinged with moral content, to the world of Wagner's first completed opera, *Die Feen*, and even beyond.

However, subtler ideas on the contact of the human and spirit worlds were also at work. Wagner can never have seen Hoffmann's opera *Undine*, and does not seem to have known the score; he would certainly have known La Motte Fouqué's famous story, though, and it may not be entirely coincidence that Hoffmann's opera ends with the lovers finding union in death in what is described as a *Liebestod. Undine* concerns the attempt of a water nymph to free herself of her spirit nature by finding marriage with a mortal, and was the most famous of various stories of similar nature. The German operas of the 1820s and 1830s were filled with settings of supernatural tales by Hoffmann, Fouqué and others, as Hanslick was to complain: 'Ghosts, goblins, witches, devils, earth and water spirits thronged the operatic stage . . . Enthusiasm for the mysteriously demonic was kindled by *Der Freischütz* and continued to demand, like a perpetually unsatisfied need, new nourishment'. This was written in connexion with *Der Vampyr* (1828), one of the operas by Heinrich Marschner which, together with *Hans Heiling* (1833) and *Der Templer und die Jüdin* (1829), Wagner conducted and much admired.

The Vampire of the opera is Lord Ruthven, a damned soul who buys extra terms of life by murdering young girls, and the plot concerns his attempts to kill three victims before midnight strikes and he must be carried off to Hell. Wagner (who even composed an extra section for one of the hero Aubry's arias) would certainly have been impressed by the scene with the second of them, the pure

Carl Perron as the Dutchman.
(Stuart-Liff Collection)

Emmy Destinn as Senta, the role in which she made her debut at Bayreuth in 1901.
(Stuart-Liff Collection)

young village girl Emmy. Fascinated by the gruesome vampire legend, she gathers her companions round her and treats them to a ballad about a vampire: *'Sieh', Mutter, dort den bleichen Mann'* ('See, Mother, over there, the pallid man'), she sings, and at the end of the song there, standing before them, is the pallid figure of Ruthven. There is an inescapable connexion between this and Senta's ballad, with its line *'Doch kann dem bleichen Manne Erlösung einstens noch werden'* (*lit.* 'There is still one chance of redemption for the pallid man.'), immediately after which the Flying Dutchman stands before her. Though Wagner professed to admire *Hans Heiling* less than *Der Vampyr*, he was influenced by some of its music in *The Ring* and he would again have encountered in it the theme of the incompatibility of the human and spirit worlds, as the gloomy, brooding earth spirit Heiling attemps to break free of his subterranean kingdom of the gnomes so as to marry an innocent young village girl.

Wagner must also have admired one of Marschner's most distinctive characteristics, the treatment of principal figures in his operas as 'anti-heroes' rather than plain villains. Already in *Euryanthe* (1823), Weber had made use, in Lysiart, of a figure torn between good and evil: one of the greatest scenes in the opera reveals him struggling to assert the nobility in his nature against the darker emotions that claim him. Bois-Guilbert, in *Der Templer und die Jüdin*, has a distinct kinship to Lysiart, and was admired by Wagner as 'a creature of the greatest originality of feeling'. He is a Knight Templar who attempts to abduct the heroine, Rebecca, but he has a nobler and more chivalric side which declares itself too late. Hans Heiling, though he attempts to interfere in the lives of the village folk and tries to kill his successful rival, eventually concedes defeat with some dignity, and is painted as a tragic rather than a wicked character. Even Ruthven, the Vampire, makes some attempt to struggle against his nature, or the unnatural force that has possessed him, and though he is portrayed as sinister and alarming,

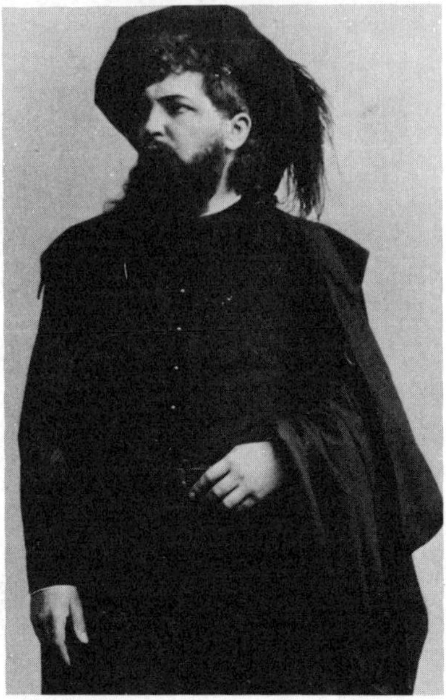

Karl Scheidermantel as the Dutchman.
(Royal College of Music)

Johannes Bischoff as the Dutchman.
(Stuart-Liff Collection)

he has a humanity that we do not meet in, say, Weber's Caspar.

These ambivalent characters clearly had much to offer Wagner when he was forming in his mind the mysterious figure of Vanderdecken. His literary sources carry little more than the seeds of such a character; and though Wagner's plot, summarised, would still suggest a ghostly visitant trying to buy his salvation at the expense of a village girl, it is evident from the Dutchman's first scene that we are in the presence of a tragic hero of larger dimensions than anything in Weber or Marschner. His emotion at Senta'a obsession with him and his decision to renounce her for her own sake are moving because they arise not from some caprice of the plot but out of a character whose stature and nobility we have come to appreciate through the music; and her final sacrifice, redeeming him with her love, is in turn true to the character of this strange, obsessed girl.

The antecedents of *The Flying Dutchman*, however, are to be sought at least as much in opéra-comique as in German Romantic opera. Already in the 18th century, French opera featured prominently in German repertories; it was to offer much to the German composers who sought the basis of a style for Romantic opera and who rejected what they regarded as the singer-dominated trivialities of Italian opera. The resistance to Italy was more of a manifesto than a fact. In the first twenty years of the 19th century the influential Leipzig *Allgemeine musikalische Zeitung* carried many articles pressing the cause of French opera as against Italian; but even Weber, vehement in his criticism of Italian 'Kling-Klang', wrote out of awareness of the strength of the Italian example (he had a reluctant admiration for Rossini), and Wagner, urging the value of fine singing upon the Germans, praised the Italian example and singled out Bellini for approval ('Bellini wrote melodies lovelier than one's dreams'). Nevertheless, it was French opéra-comique which provided the creative basis for German Romantic opera, in numerous ways. The increased role of the orchestra, especially to depict natural scenery and events; the development thereby made possible of the old Reminiscence Motive into something approaching Leitmotiv; the tendency to move away from separate numbers into a more continuous process of development by self-contained scenes merging arioso and aria – these are but some of the characteristics that held much for German composers in general, and for Wagner in particular. From Méhul, whose work Wagner regarded as significant and of whom, according to Cosima, he spoke constantly, he must have appreciated the effectiveness of allowing natural forces, including the sea, to play an integral role in the drama through the orchestra. Méhul's use of motifs must also have interested him; and it is perhaps particularly from the example of Méhul and Cherubini that there grew the ability to merge an introduction and an aria into something almost seamless (as with the Dutchman's opening '*Die Frist ist um*') and in turn to draw such self-contained scenes into groups as the structural basis of the entire opera. It is a commonplace that the step from *Rienzi* (1842) to *The Flying Dutchman* (1843) was one of the largest in Wagner's career; it also marks a turn from the influence of French Grand Opera, as cultivated by Spontini and Auber, to that of opéra-comique.

Not that Wagner forgot any of the lessons he learnt from Auber. He regarded *La Muette de Portici* as the first appearance of true music drama, and the work's concentration of arias, duets and so on into a single form he particularly praised in his essay *Erinnerungen an Auber*: 'one can scarcely distinguish arias and duets in the usual manner of opera ... the recitatives seem like streaks of lightning; one moves from the recitatives to the choral ensembles as if in a storm, and in the middle of this frenzied chaos come suddenly still more energetic exhortations to calm or repeated calls of a new furious intoxication ...'. He had scarcely less admiration for Boieldieu's most famous work, *La Dame blanche*, which he regarded as 'a model of what the French spirit can produce'. It was an opera that held particular associations for him, as it was not only one of the first works he heard in Leipzig but the one in which, during his time as chorus master in Würzburg, his brother Albert had made his début as George Brown. His admiration for the effect of Jenny's ballad was another contribution, together with Emmy's in *Der Vampyr*, to Senta's ballad and its dramatic placing; and he often expressed approval of the spinning scene – as well he might, since there is not only a comparable effect in *The Flying Dutchman* but even a phrase exactly cribbed. He praised the work for its 'symbolic Romanticism'.

Ironically, the Grand Opera style that had won Wagner such a success with *Rienzi* in Dresden in 1842 militated against *The Flying Dutchman* in the following year. The Dresdeners, delighted with the grandiose manner of *Rienzi* and undeterred by its enormous length, were disconcerted by what they saw as a reversion to an older, even a quainter, German Romanticism. As often with a powerfully imaginative new work, the superfices were more easily grasped than the true originality; and there were few who realised the music's real quality. Berlioz, who saw a performance, was a little reserved, impressed by 'the sombre colouring of the music and by some remarkable effects of storm and wind which are an integral part of the dramatic character of the work': he was irritated by the excess of tremolo, which he regarded as 'intellectual laziness' – a charge rare among the many that were to be levelled at Wagner's head.

How much the performance was to blame for the work's muted effect, it is hard to say. Wagner was full of praise for his admired Wilhelmine Schröder-Devrient, the singer whose dramatic power had first aroused in him the urge to compose, but very reserved about Johann Wächter as the Dutchman. Berlioz found her less impressive, complaining of 'affected poses and the spoken phrases that she finds it necessary to interject thoughout the role' (it must be said that other accounts of her at this stage of her career tend to support Berlioz); Wächter was, Berlioz thought, 'a really remarkable and unspoiled talent'. However, the crucial role of the orchestra remains more mysterious. The leader, Karl Lipinski, was a friend of Berlioz, and much admired by him; Wagner was less impressed, finding Lipinski too much of a virtuoso and too wilful for the leader of what he sought, — a harmonious, thoroughly blended ensemble, such as his predecessor Weber had striven for. Wagner's strictures on Weber's successor Reissiger need not be taken at face value, but for all his care for standards Reissiger seems to have found difficulty in raising the level of the Dresden orchestra to the point at which it was really competent to deal with so demanding a score as Wagner's. Orchestrally, *Rienzi* is conventional beside *The Flying Dutchman*; though the Dresden orchestra had quite a good reputation by contemporary standards, it can scarcely have been up to the demands of the new score. Berlioz reported that one of the bass players was too old even to hold up his instrument; and the lack of general discipline permitted one of the oboe players to decorate his part according to his own taste. Other accounts suggest that the resources of the Dresden house, while adequate to the general repertory and capable, it seems, of rising to the occasion of *Rienzi*, was too uneven to do full justice to *The Flying Dutchman.* The seedy old bass player was given support by the leader of the cellos, one of the great players of his day, Friedrich Dotzauer; and Berlioz was delighted with the cor anglais player. No-one dissents from the view that Wagner conducted with energy and precision. A few in the city were to sense the bold new ideas that dominated, and made something new of, all that had gone into the formation of the work; but in 1843 its day had not yet come.

Friedrich Schorr, a very fine Dutchman heard at Covent Garden between the wars.

Kirsten Flagstad 'A heroically radiant Senta' at Covent Garden in 1937.

An Introduction to 'The Flying Dutchman'

John Deathridge

Scotsmen may (or may not) be pleased to hear that Wagner's *Flying Dutchman* was originally set in Scotland. In the manuscript score of the opera preserved in the Bayreuth archives the place of the action is described as 'the Scottish coast'. Senta's fiancé is a huntsman called 'Georg'. The name of her father is 'Donald', a skipper whose ship is manned by 'Scottish' sailors. The ship drops anchor in the opening scene of the opera near a coastal village with the Scottish-sounding name of 'Holystrand'. And Wagner's skipper greets the Dutchman in the third scene with the line, '*Gastfreundschaft kennt der Schotte*' (literally: 'The Scotsman knows hospitality').

Two months before the Dresden première of the *Dutchman* on January 2, 1843, Wagner changed the location of the opera from Scotland to Norway. The decision caused him a lot of work: not only did he have to go through the entire score changing the names of the characters and many of the stage directions, he also had to alter the vocal scores and many of the cues in the orchestral parts which had already been copied for the rehearsals. It is not out of the question that some of the singers actually learnt their parts *à l'écossais*; and it is certainly not impossible that the production was being geared to show something of the wild Scottish landscape familiar to German audiences from countless plays and novels popular at the time.

Why did Wagner make the change at such a late stage? Were German opera-goers tired of Scotland? Did they prefer Scandinavian names like Sandwike and Erik (instead of Holystrand and Georg) with those striking "k"s to make them look Norwegian? Or was Wagner simply disguising his debt to Marschner and Heine? After all, Marschner's opera *The Vampire* (1827) also takes place in Scotland. It even has a similar constellation of characters, one of whom, like Senta's fiancé, happens to be a huntsman called Georg. Heine, too, allows his Flying Dutchman (in the seventh chapter of his *Memoirs of Mr von Schnabelewopski*) to come ashore in Scotland where he meets a 'Scottish businessman'. And of course both Marschner and Heine knew how to exploit the typical Romantic passion for Scotland with its eerie castles, raw landscape and general air of mystery.

The most likely reason for Wagner's decision, however, is that he wanted to heighten the autobiographical significance of the *Dutchman*. Only a few weeks after the première he published his first excursion into the art of self-profile. It was a substantial essay called *Autobiographical Sketch* (February, 1843) and contained a vivid account of a hazardous voyage along the Norwegian coast-line which Wagner had undertaken on his way to Paris shortly before beginning work on the *Dutchman*. What could have been more effective than to give the opera a similar atmosphere? 'The voyage through the Norwegian reefs', Wagner wrote, 'made a wonderful impression on my imagination; the legend of the Flying Dutchman, which the sailors verified, took on a distinctive, strange colouring that only my sea adventures could have given it.'

*

If the idea of moving the *Dutchman* from Scotland to Norway was one of the young Wagner's most brilliant autobiographical *coups de théâtre*, it is not surprising that the mature Wagner reinterpreted the opera to make it conform to his later theories. His ingenuity in creating an apparent unity between (German) art and (German) life was matched only by his equally ingenious attempts to see his early works, particularly the *Dutchman*, as precursors of the music drama. One of the most famous and influential passages in this vein comes from his essay *A Communication to My Friends* (1851) which was written while he was at work on the libretto of the *Ring*:

> Before I actually worked out *The Flying Dutchman* in detail, I remember sketching out Senta's Ballad in the second Act and composing the verse and melody to it in full. I had unconsciously laid the thematic foundation of the entire music of the opera in this piece . . . When I eventually got down to work on the composition, the thematic idea I had already conceived began to spread itself like a complete net over the entire drama.

Senta's Ballad is certainly dramatically central to the *Dutchman*. But no impartial listener could describe it as the musical plasma from which the rest of the opera grew. Nor could he hear its themes as a net cast 'over the entire drama' without an exceptional leap of acoustical faith. Wagner is being tendentious, too, when he suggests that Senta's Ballad was the first number to be composed. What he does not say is that, before writing the libretto of the *Dutchman* in 1841, he wrote three songs from the opera for a Paris audition in the previous year: Senta's Ballad, the Norwegian Sailors' Song in Act Three ('Steersman leave the watch!') and the so-called Phantom Song or *Spukgesang* sung by the Dutchman's crew in the same scene. Any one of these pieces could have had musical priority. All three were composed at the same time and were obviously intended as operatic 'numbers' in the traditional sense. As we shall see, their musical and dramatic significance was by no means limited to Senta's Ballad.

The supreme irony of Wagner's later interpretation is that he overlooked the virtues of his own music. Like many writers who have taken his words at face value, he came to believe that the *Dutchman* was a closely integrated network of organically related themes. In fact, the opera tends to go in the opposite direction. What makes it so effective is not the sophisticated leitmotif system of, say, the *Ring*, but a rumbustious ragbag of disparate elements that sounds quite unlike the seamless textures of the mature music dramas. The *Dutchman* is full of violent contrasts, grisly orchestration*, simple tunes, huge leaps from one style to another, and a host of stock techniques used with originality and panache. Although Wagner does make use of the so-called 'reminiscence motif' (the recall of telling musical phrases associated with specific moods or characters), his application of it in the opera is sporadic and without the subtle complexity of his later music.

The real musical and dramatic crux of the *Dutchman* is the verse song. Two of Wagner's later works, *Tannhäuser* and *The Mastersingers*, are famous examples of the use of song (i.e. the actual act of singing) as a dramatic symbol or metaphor. The Song to Venus sung by the protagonist in *Tannhäuser* and Walther's Prize Song in *The Mastersingers* both have extra-musical ambitions that are meant to convey the idealism of the artist or the glories of German Art. And Wagner

* Especially in Wagner's use of the wind instruments, the orchestration of the *Dutchman* shows the unmistakable influence of Berlioz and Mendelssohn — two composers whom the mature Wagner regarded publicly with unpleasant condescension. Wagner admitted privately to the London critic Eduard Dannreuther that he had made a 'detailed study' of Berlioz's orchestration in *Romeo and Juliet* as early as 1840, the year in which he composed the three numbers from the *Dutchman* for a Paris audition. He later presented a copy of the first edition of *Tristan* to Berlioz which is now in the Bibliothèque Nationale in Paris. The dedication reads: 'To the great and esteemed composer of *Romeo and Juliet*'.

cleverly distinguishes between the song as a dramatic object and the 'normal' singing that surrounds it by using a realistic frame: the organisation of a formal competition or 'War of Song' (*Sängerkrieg*) in *Tannhäuser*, and Walther's 'lesson' with Hans Sachs in *The Mastersingers* in which he learns how to shape the Prize Song according to the rules of true art.

Wagner's use of song in the *Dutchman* is hardly less important. Although without any conspicuous cultural message, his treatment of the song forms in the opera ingeniously expresses the tension between normality and mystery central to the work. There are five songs in all: the Steersman's Song in Act One; the Spinning Chorus and Senta's Ballad in Act Two; and the two songs of the Norwegian sailors and the Dutchman's crew in Act Three. What sets them apart as songs in the literal sense, as opposed to the 'normal' singing that makes up the rest of the opera, is that they are inevitably interrupted by a real event. Indeed, the unfinished songs of the *Dutchman* could be seen as a striking, and uncannily precise metaphor for the frustrated passion of the protagonist. The Steersman falls asleep like the dormouse in *Alice in Wonderland*. Senta breaks off the spinning chorus by telling it to 'stop that stupid song' (a remark that delighted Wagner's critics). The song of the Norwegian sailors is interupted by *another* song, the Phantom Song of the Dutchman's crew. And Senta leaves her Ballad unfinished by breaking off the third refrain with a text of her own in the first person: 'I do, and I shall be the one to save you! Angel of God bring us together! Through me you shall be saved!'

*

Overture.

The *Dutchman* Overture is the best proof (if any were needed) that the songs of the opera are central to its musical conception. Although it was written last in the later summer of 1841, the Overture consists mainly of ideas drawn from the three songs set to music for the Paris audition in 1840 which were the first sections of the work to be composed.*

The first group of themes is taken from the Phantom Song of the Dutchman's crew [1, 2, 3]. And like that song, the music launches almost at once into a series of giddy movements that quickly obscure the opening key. After a short time in which a lot seems to happen, we hear a virile theme taken from the Dutchman's monologue in Act One [4] which soon subsides into the gentle refrain of Senta's Ballad [5]. Wagner never tired of comparing these 'masculine' and 'feminine' elements in the opera with Faust and Gretchen in Goethe's famous play. The idea, of course, is really an astonishing piece of musical cunning. The shock of the opening heightens the plaintive melody of the Ballad; having dazzled our ears with violent sounds, Wagner beguiles them with the sweet and sentimental. The stylistic contrast could not be greater. Nor could it sum up the vigorous emotion of the whole opera to better effect.

The rest of the Overture is a potpourri of themes and sounds from the song of the Norwegian sailors [10, 11], Senta's Ballad [5, 8] and the wild cries of the Dutchman's crew [2, 7] bound together by snatches from the Dutchman's monologue [4, 6, 9]. Wagner concludes with yet another brilliant stroke that is the

* Another sign that the Overture was in Wagner's mind at an early stage is the resemblance between its opening and the beginning of Beethoven's Ninth Symphony. According to Wagner's own accounts, this work made a profound impression on him during the first months of his Paris sojourn. It therefore seems likely that he deliberately converted the mysterious bare fifths of Beethoven's opening into the rasping sound of the open fifths at the beginning of the *Dutchman* Overture (Example 1) – the "salty breeze" which Franz Liszt claimed to hear in the piece.

essence of the opera. Instead of finishing with one of the songs, as we might expect, he builds the conclusion around the theme which Senta sings when she *interrupts* her Ballad [12]. It is as if the upward rush of the violins that introduces the final section were to wrench the Overture from the conditional into the present tense. The change of key from D minor to D major, too, creates a mood of affirmation – the transformation of a remote world into a physical reality.

Act One

No. 1. Introduction.

Because so many good things happen later in the *Dutchman*, the mastery of its opening scene has often been overlooked. The scene is built around the cries of the Norwegian sailors [13, 14] and the Steersman's Song. Between these colourful figures Wagner inserted the prosaic figure of Daland (Senta's father) who sings some appropriately four-square music. Ernest Newman once criticized Wagner for giving Daland some monotonous melodies, including his first arioso [16]. But Newman gave little credit to Wagner's dramatic instinct. Daland's music may be sometimes dull when seen in isolation; but in the context of the sailors' and the Steersman's songs, not to mention the whistling of the wind expressed by a short figure played by the piccolo [15], the effect is exactly right. Daland is the epitome of normality. Why shouldn't his music be unexceptional too?

The centre-point of the scene is the Steersman's Song. It is introduced by a wide-leaping tune [17] alternating with the rushing of the violas and cellos. We can already sense what is going to happen: the Steersman is fighting his tiredness and the waves are beginning to move in anticipation of the Dutchman's arrival. The song is built around two memorable themes [18, 19] and its first verse concludes with a violent movement of the waves portrayed by thumping timpani and strings alternating with jagged wind chords. Once Wagner has imprinted the full context of the song on our ears, he uses it a second time to create a specific effect. The technique is as simple as it is ingenious. All Wagner does is to space out the phrases of the second verse so that the gaps become longer and longer. Thus he not only gives us a musical description of how the Steersman falls asleep, but also fills the ever-widening spaces with disturbing sounds which vividly portray the arrival of the Dutchman's ship. By the time the Steersman loses control of his tiredness, the last fragment of his song has vanished and the Dutchman steps ashore.

No. 2. Aria

The Dutchman's monologue begins with a grinding figure in the violas and cellos which expresses his desperate mood exactly [20]. Wagner was a master of concision. If you don't believe this, just listen carefully to this opening. Note how Wagner builds the phrase around the interval of the diminished fifth or tritone E sharp/B, which is echoed by the horn in the second bar. What could be a more precise musical description of the Dutchman's demonic aura? And if you are puzzled by the term 'diminished fifth', you may be interested to know that it is an interval which medieval theorists referred to as the 'Devil in Music' (*diabolus in musica*). Even in the Romantic Age, it never quite lost its bad reputation.

The opening recitative of the monologue builds in intensity until it tumbles into a long aria. In contrast to the 'organic' view of the *Dutchman* music encouraged by the mature Wagner, the three main themes of the aria have little to do with one another [21, 22, 23]. In fact, the music thrives on abrupt changes and manic repetitions that propel it forward. There is little formal repetition; and

Example 1. The opening bars of Beethoven's Ninth Symphony (above) and The Flying Dutchman overture. See footnote

when it does occur it only serves to confirm the sense of endless chaos. The intensity of the aria seems futile because its thematic disunity is really what holds it together. And once again Wagner beautifully summarizes this dramatic and musical paradox with a remote and spine-chilling vignette. As the monologue draws to its close, the music moves unexpectedly from C minor into the distant key of E minor. The Dutchman's crew sings the short but telling phrase '*Ewige Vernichtung nimm' uns auf*' ('Endless oblivion I am yours'), and the music, just as unexpectedly, returns quickly to C minor. It is a fleeting touch that exactly mirrors the aria's disruptive mood.

No. 3. Scene, Duet and Chorus

Daland wakes his sleepy Steersman who sings another snatch from the second

An unidentified early set for the first act. (Royal College of Music)

verse of his song. At the end of the scene the Norwegian sailors add another verse to the same song. Thus the whole scene, and the entire first Act, appear to be in a surrounding frame consisting of the Steersman's Song. The events of the present scene (and the preceding monologue of the Dutchman) are in parenthesis, so to speak, between the second and the third verse.

When Daland eventually notices the Dutchman, Wagner introduces a crawling phrase on the lower strings [24]. Again it is a precise musical description of what is happening: the Dutchman is seeking shelter and wants to persuade Daland to give it to him. The phrase is recalled again and again as the Dutchman gives Daland a self-pitying account of his fateful journeys. Its inevitable return to the same upper note is a painful negation that expresses the vicious circle in which the Dutchman finds himself. The following duet, too, is a good example of Wagner's knack of finding suitable musical metaphors to reflect specific situations. The Dutchman sings in long cantilenas while Daland gloats over the possibility of doing business with him in short snappy phrases reminiscent of French comic opera. When Daland reveals that he has a daughter he could offer to the Dutchman, his words are introduced with a short phrase [25] that is a glaring contrast to the pessimism of the Dutchman's music. It may not be one of Wagner's most 'inspired' musical ideas; but its sharp rhythm and regular upward movement could be seen as a clever stylistic symbol of Daland's banal optimism.

Transition

At the end of Act One the Norwegian sailors raise the anchor of their ship and

The 1966 Covent Garden production, designed by Sean Kenny, produced by Clifford Williams (photo: Donald Southern)

Norman Bailey as the Dutchman in the 1975 BBC2 production: the first time a complete Wagner opera was given in a television studio performance.

Gwyneth Jones by the statue of the Dutchman used in the BBC2 production (1975) (BBC copyright photographs)

hoist the sails. According to Wagner's directions the scene must then change as quickly as possible. The musical transition mirrors the transformation ingeniously with a lilting two-note motif taken from the Song of the Norwegian Sailors [14] that literally weaves its way into the Spinning Song [26] at the beginning of Act Two. Wagner has made it clear in the Overture that this motif is derived from a single bar in Senta's Ballad (compare [5a] fourth bar, [8], [14] and [26]). Thus within the short space of the transition he spins a thematic thread that connects together three songs central to the opera, two of which appear in the following scene. This is not part of the mythical network of themes he later claimed to have cast 'over the entire drama'. It is rather that the songs form a group which, precisely because of its inner connectedness, stands out in sharp relief against the rest of the work. Wagner is matching single pieces of dramatic and musical clothing, not an entire wardrobe.

Act Two

No. 4. Song, Scene, Ballad and Chorus

The breezy A major of the Spinning Song [26] that opens this scene is intended as

Hans Hotter as the Dutchman (Met. Archives)

Viorica Ursuleac as Senta (Ida Cook Collection)

a direct contrast with, and at the same time a formal parallel to, the minor key of Senta's Ballad [27] that follows it. The Ballad is usually sung in G minor. In Wagner's manuscript score, however, it is in A minor; and although the link with the Spinning Song is hardly impaired by the transposition, the apposition of A major and A minor in the original version is clearly significant.

Many composers from Mozart and Schubert to Mahler were fond of blending a major chord or key into a minor one with the same root. You can try out the effect on the piano by playing a simple chord of A major followed immediately by A minor. The contrast of mood could not be greater or more simply achieved. Indeed, Wagner was to base large sections of a later work, *Lohengrin*, on exactly the same effect. In the original version of the *Dutchman*, too, the light-hearted A major of the Spinning Song is gradually merged into the melancholy A minor of Senta's Ballad. Both songs have three verses and are interrupted by Senta for profoundly different reasons. Thus a larger form emerges that embraces both pieces and the entire scene too. Wagner completes the form by returning to A major for the final chorus. The tune is jolly and deliberately superficial [28] – another almost devilish imitation of French comic opera. Its hysterical mood is appropriate: after the magic of Senta's Ballad the 'normal' world of everyday routine is never quite the same again.

No. 5. Duet

The centre-point of the duet between Senta and Erik is the so-called Dream Narration. Although the *Dutchman* is hardly a fledgling music drama as the mature Wagner tended to think, this scene is certainly a premonition of his later interest (via Schopenhauer) in dreams and the unconscious. Indeed, soon after the first performance he added a suggestive stage direction to the duet that implies

Annie Krull as Senta (Royal College of Music)

Ernestine Schumann-Heink as Mary (Met. Archives)

at least a passing acquaintance with the ideas of Mesmer and Puységur – two early pioneers in the discovery of the unconscious whose work greatly interested the German Romantics.* The direction reads: 'At the beginning of Erik's Narration Senta sinks into a magnetic sleep and appears to dream the dream that Erik is telling her' (1843/4). The significance of this is that Wagner created the dramatic situation before he rationalized it. In the original manuscript score we read simply that 'Senta approaches Erik'. But the text and the music already suggest that Senta is mesmerized by Erik's vision. The new direction is merely a more telling visual realization of the composer's aural imagination. Like the Dream Narration itself, Wagner's fantasy was ahead of reality.

Wagner prepares the Dream Narration with characteristic skill. The hapless Erik is bursting to tell Senta of his woes. Appropriately, Wagner gives him a short-breathed melody [29] that refuses to unfold – actually a technical shortcoming which he turned to precise dramatic advantage. The very awkwardness of Erik's music is astonishingly effective. Its broken structure is not only a reflection of his lack of skill in expressing himself, it is also a subborn contrast to the taught continuous texture of the following narration.

In an irrational outburst, Erik accuses Senta of being ensnared by Satan, and

* Readers interested in the history of psychology may like to know that the *Dutchman* was one of Wagner's works that attracted the attention of Freud's circle in Vienna during its early years. The small group that met regularly in Freud's house to discuss his ideas admittedly concentrated more on the biographical significance of the *Dutchman* than on its contribution to the theory of dreams. Nevertheless, a paper entitled *Richard Wagner in 'The Flying Dutchman'* read to the circle by Max Graf throws new light on the character of Erik (who does not appear in Heine's account of the story) and Wagner's reasons for inventing him. Those who read German can find the paper in the ninth volume of *Schriften zur angewandten Seelenkunde*, edited by Siegmund Freud, Leipzig 1911.

almost the entire orchestra answers his diminished fifth (the 'Devil in Music') with a frenetic repetition of a single chord [30]. The Dream Narration begins. Senta listens spellbound to Erik, recreating each detail of his dream of how her father brings a mysterious stranger to the house. But when Erik relates his vision of her fleeing with the stranger across the ocean, she awakens abruptly. Her 'magnetic sleep' is interrupted by the realistic thought that *she* is the woman the stranger is looking for. Senta retreats into her imagination once more and sings the remaining few bars of the Ballad omitted in the previous scene [5b]. Even this fragment is left incomplete: instead of singing the final note she utters a cry of fright as her father enters with the Dutchman. Erik's dream is now a reality.

No. 6. Finale – Aria, Duet and Trio

If Senta's Ballad and Erik's Dream Narration tell exciting stories about the Dutchman which are full of adventure and euphoric detail, his actual presence on the stage is surprisingly sober. He enters to the accompaniment of the timpani alone [31] – one of those ominous pulsations that Wagner never tired of using to create low-key tension. He is followed by Daland who sings a business-as-usual aria based on a pretty melody with a distinct flavour of Berlioz [32]. Characteristically, Wagner never develops the tune with the suavity it deserves. The music keeps stopping and starting as if something were amiss with Daland's calculations. And as usual Wagner's aural instincts are right. Senta is attracted to the Dutchman as Daland anticipated; but there is a tension between them he does not understand. Surprised and perplexed, he leaves.

For singers and listeners alike, the following duet between Senta and the Dutchman is one of the most exhausting numbers in the opera. Although full of Italianate melody and French-like orchestration, it sounds heavy-handed. Even the verve of the concluding theme [33] fails to enliven the Dutchman's laboured advances and Senta's righteous avowal of faith unto death. Only the return of Senta's father saves the situation. In an influential introduction to the *Dutchman*, Liszt wrote that he regretted Wagner's undercutting of the passionate thrust of

Leonie Rysanek as Senta. (Stuart-Liff Collection)

Set Svanholm as Erik at the Met. (Met. Archives)

the music with the prosaic reappearance of Daland. Liszt misunderstood Wagner's dramatic strategy: if the second Act had ended with a love duet, the tension between fantasy and reality central to the opera would have been weakened. Daland interrupts the duet with a march-like theme [34] that brings us down to earth with a jolt. The 'ideal' world of Senta and the Dutchman is never quite the same again.

Transition

The scene changes from a room in Daland's house to the bay outside where the ship of the Norwegians, full of life and bright festivity, is seen alongside the sinister darkness of the Dutchman's vessel. The transition is built mainly from the introductory tune to the Steersman's song [17] and snatches from the Song of the Norwegian Sailors [10, 11, 14] that opens the third Act.

Act Three

No. 7. Chorus and Ensemble

From a structural and orchestral point of view this scene is one of the most inventive in the opera. Wagner's virtuosity in combining and distending various sounds to portray the growing excitement of the Norwegians as they try to goad some life out of the Dutchman's crew is without precedent in his early works. His

The Dutchman's spectral crew terrify the Norwegian sailors in the 1982 ENO production by David Pountney, designed by Stefanos Lazaridis. (photo: Reg Wilson)

use of song, too, is even more ingenious than in previous scenes.

The Norwegian sailors sing three verses of their song. After the first verse there is a merry interlude during which the sailors and their girl-friends taunt the Dutchman's crew. Wagner throws a musical shadow of unease over the festivities with the introductory tune of the Steersman's Song in the minor key [35], some daring harmonic effects [36] and the transformation of a motif from the Phantom Song of the Dutchman's crew into another diminished fifth, or 'Devil in Music' [37]. By the time the sailors sing the second verse of their song the mysterious ship is beginning to show signs of movement. The jittery orchestration betrays the growing fear of the Norwegians whose song in C major is now interrupted by the Phantom Song of the Dutchman's crew in the remote key of B minor. The ghostly sailors sing two fearsome verses. And Wagner's crowning act of musical and theatrical mastery arrives when he combines the third verses of both songs in two different and remotely related keys. The Norwegians are reduced to silence by the wild apparition; and with a loud cry of raucous laughter the Phantom Song of the Dutchman's crew disintegrates.

No. 8. Duet, Cavatine, Finale

Erik enters with Senta in great agitation. In an impassioned duet he implores her in vain not to uphold her vow of eternal fidelity to the Dutchman. The vicious circle in which Erik and Senta are entwined is reflected by two motifs [38, 39] that are repeated incessantly without development. Like the short phrase used to express the Dutchman's futile existence in his first confrontation with Daland in Act One [24] both figures have a tendency to negate themselves by returning to the same upper note. The music creates an atmosphere of hopelessnes and coming disaster. Even the simple honesty of Erik's Cavatine [40] cannot change Senta's decision. Her bond with the Dutchman is inviolable.

When the Dutchman sees and overhears Erik and Senta together he immediately assumes that Senta has been unfaithful to him. Deeply disappointed he boards his ship and departs. Nevertheless, Senta's bond with him and the sinister world he represents is unshaken. While Senta's counterpart in Marschner's opera *The Vampire* marries her middle-class fiancé after breaking with the demonic forces that have enticed her, Senta remains true to her vow of eternal fidelity to the Dutchman by committing suicide. Wagner borrowed the idea from

Eva van der Osten as Senta (Stuart-Liff Collection)

Heine who pointed the moral of the tale with exquisite irony: 'women must be careful of marrying a Flying Dutchman; and we men can see from the piece how, in the best of circumstances, women are the ruin of us all'. But Wagner preferred a less conventional and more ambiguous ending. Senta and Erik are neither drawn closer together by their escapade with the supernatural, nor is the redemption of the Dutchman by Senta's suicide framed by sceptical common sense. Wagner combines the typical happy-end of romantic opera with the tragic conclusion of French grand opera; and to do this he had to reject both Heine's seemingly amoral wit and Marschner's bland respectability. The Dutchman is freed from the curse upon him and Senta from her petty existence among small-minded spinners and worthy huntsmen. But Senta's relationship with Erik is destroyed, and her family and friends are left in disarray. As the Dutchman rises 'transfigured' above the ocean with Senta in his arms, Wagner's music makes it easy to forget that the demonic has triumphed.

*

When Wagner moved the setting of the *Dutchman* from Scotland to Norway, it was only the first of many alterations he made to the work. For the first performances he transposed Senta's Ballad into G minor and relinquished the idea of playing the three Acts of the opera without an interval. He undertook major revisions of the orchestration in 1846, and again in 1852 when he retouched the instrumentation of the ending of the Overture. For a performance in Weimar in 1853 he expressly asked Liszt, who was to conduct the opera, to change the orchestration of a single chord: the accompaniment of Senta's cry at the beginning of the second Act Finale. For his Paris concerts in 1860 he made two major additions to the ending of the Overture and added a harp to its orchestration. He even began a completely new version of Senta's Ballad (a sketch of which has survived) for a model performance of the *Dutchman* in Munich for King Ludwig. In the 1870's too, he told his publishers that he intended to revise the opera further before having the full score engraved. Cosima's Diaries report on April 9, 1880, that Wagner 'wants to postpone the dictation of the Autobiography until after the performance of *Parsifal* when he also wants to . . . rearrange *The Flying Dutchman*'. And as late as September 8, 1881, just one-and-a-half years before Wagner's death, Cosima writes: 'At tea-time Richard talks about *The Flying Dutchman* and tells me that it makes him sad to find in it so much noisiness and so many repetitions that damage the work'.

Wagner was preoccupied at regular intervals with the *Dutchman* for a major part of his life. Although he never found time to give posterity a final 'definitive' version, it is perhaps possible to deduce something of what he had in mind from his revision of the ending of the Overture in 1860. The ending (like the ending of the whole opera) is built around the theme that Senta sings when she interrupts her Ballad [12]. For his Paris concerts Wagner added 21 bars in the style of *Tristan* and allowed the refrain of the Ballad [5] to sound once more in the concluding bars. Not only the music, but also its dramatic point were therefore given a new flavour. Instead of remaining outside the Ballad in the triumphant-sounding key of D major, the new ending takes a leap backwards into the meditative atmosphere of the song with chromatic modulations, the evocative sound of the harp, and the final quotation from the Ballad itself. This version, which is usually the one that is played today, assumes a more introspective character that smooths over the raw vitality of the original. Why did Wagner make the change? Did he, like Senta, want to turn fantasy into reality by recomposing the music to make it fit his later interpretation of the *Dutchman* as a potential music drama? Or did he simply want to improve the opera's lack of technical sophistication? We shall never know. But the hybrid style of the revisions he did make at least tend to show that the work is not the inherently German precursor of the music drama that Wagner wanted posterity to think it was. Despite his attempts to change it, the *Dutchman* has stubbornly remained a vigorous and refreshingly cosmopolitan opera that was originally conceived for Paris, first performed in Germany, influenced by French, German and Italian music – and originally set in Scotland.

Otakar Kraus as the Dutchman.

Loneliness, Love and Death

William Vaughan

> *The form of The Flying Dutchman* is the mythical poem of the folk: a primeval trait of man's essential nature is expressed here with overwhelming power. This trait, in its widest sense, is the longing for peace from life's storms. — Wagner.

It is usually in their early works that artists reveal their roots most clearly. *The Flying Dutchman* is no exception. The theme, even more than the music, is steeped in the cultural preoccupations of the nineteenth century. To some extent this was deliberate. At the time Wagner was desperately seeking to establish his reputation and undoubtedly he chose the subject with an eye to its popular appeal. But this is only half the story. Wagner was, as well, genuinely fascinated by the implications of the legend, and identified strongly with them.

The legend had already attracted considerable attention before Wagner chose it for his opera. He based his libretto on the version that had appeared in the poet Heinrich Heine's *Salon* in 1834. The story had first appeared in print in 1821 in *Blackwood's Magazine*, and many forms of it were subsequently published in France, England and Germany.

The legend itself is older. The figure of Vanderdecken as such — the Dutchman in Spanish costume — suggests a date in the seventeenth century. The folklorist R. Engert* has, however, pointed out features which would indicate that this is just an adaptation of a theme of greater antiquity. The fatal oath made by the Dutchman — to round the Cape of Good Hope even if this should take him to the Day of Judgement — is similar to one said to have been made by the great Portuguese explorer Vasco da Gama in 1498 when he rounded the Cape for the first time. The fear of the ordinary sailor at the intrepid nature of Gama and other Renaissance explorers may well have inspired the original legend. But it may go back further even than this, to a much earlier group of seamen adventurers — the Vikings.

The interest in recording and elaborating it in the early nineteenth century reflects the current vogue for folk tales; a vogue which we must thank for having stimulated many magnificent collections including the works of the Brothers Grimm. In Germany folk literature had taken on particular significance. Already in the middle of the previous century the writer J.G. Herder had emphasized how it enshrined the imaginative power and closeness to nature of primitive peoples. Later writers — notably the poet Novalis — were fascinated by the way in which the fantasy of the folk tale embodied levels of experience normally closed to more rational discourse. With their great interest in reviving national culture many German Romantic artists had drawn upon both the forms and themes of folk literature, and Wagner inherited this concern for the national and psychological dimensions of myth. In the case of the 'mythical poem' *The Flying Dutchman*, it is the pyschological, rather than the national, that predominates.

Even before it was written down, the Flying Dutchman legend had made its impact on literature. For English readers the most notable instance is Coleridge's *Ancient Mariner* (1798). Although Coleridge's poem is far from a simple reworking of the legend, it shares the central theme of a sailor condemned to continuous wandering for a blasphemy. There may also be a specific reference to

* *'Die Sage vom Fliegenden Holländer'*, *Meereskunde*, Bd. 13, 7. Heft 173, *Berlin*, 1927.

the Dutchman legend in the description of the death ship that appears after the mariner has shot the albatross and he and his comrades are stricken with thirst. For, in the traditional version of the legend, the Dutchman's ship brings death or misfortune to those who encounter her.

As J. Dickson Lowes suggested in *The Road to Xanadu*, Coleridge presumably came across the legend amongst the sea folk of the West Country where he was living at the time. But like Wagner he appears to have been encouraged to rework it by the example of German poets. Like Goethe, Schiller and Gottfried Bürger, he aimed to emulate the simple, rhythmic structure of folk ballads, and shared their interest in developing the fantasy and emotional elements in the traditional stories. In the case of the Dutchman this was to lead to an important shift of emphasis. In the legend the Dutchman is no hero but a warning against the consequences of breaking the natural law. In the Romantic treatments of the theme, by contrast, he is viewed with sympathy. The painfulness of his punishment is dwelt upon, and the possibility of his salvation is entertained.

A similar change can be found at the time in the attitude to other traditional stories where the protagonist defies the will of God. In all there is a fascination with the fate of the protagonist, with the way he moved beyond normal experience, often wandering through vast dimensions of space or time. The quest for limitless experience seemed to take on a justification of its own. The most celebrated of these legends were, of course, *Faust* — the scholar who sold his soul to the devil for a share of supernatural power, and *Don Juan* — the libertine who would stop at no lengths in his pursuit of the erotic. These works were in everyone's minds at the time, having formed the basis of masterpieces by Goethe, Mozart and Byron. *Faust* was particularly in Wagner's mind when he was composing his opera, and he had, in fact, just completed a *Faust* overture that presages the musical style of the *Dutchman*. The concept of Vanderdecken's release from his curse through the faithful love of Senta obviously parallels the conclusion of Goethe's poem, where Faust is redeemed through the intercession of Gretchen. The idea that the Dutchman was saved through the love of a woman had been an innovation of Heine's, which may have been intended as a deliberate satire on Goethe's work. Be that as it may, the innovation was seized upon by Wagner and developed with eagerness.

Faust, Don Juan and the Flying Dutchman appealed to the Romantics as rebels. Of the three, however, the Dutchman is the only one whose punishment — rather than crime — forms the focus of the story. Where Faust and Don Juan wander at will, in a constant search for new adventure, the Dutchman wanders only because he is seeking the peace of death. Even the addition of the notion of his salvation through the love of a woman does not detract from the isolation and emptiness of his meanderings across the ocean.

The loneliness of the Dutchman is at the heart of the legend. R. Engert has suggested that this expresses the basic predicament of the sailor, who sails in order to reach land, but has no purpose when he gets there but to set out to sea again. This certainly explains why it developed so powerfully amongst sailors — particularly amongst those of Northern Europe who had become accustomed to undertaking voyages of long duration. When the legend was taken up by the Romantics this loneliness took on new dimensions. In an age when the artist came increasingly to see his role as that of the outsider, independent of conventional society, it seemed that he must necessarily suffer the burden of isolation as payment for the originality of his vision. *'L'indépendance a pour conséquence l'isolement'*, wrote the French author Benjamin Constant in his autobiographical novel *Adolphe* (1816).

Design by Emil Preetorius for the 1939 Bayreuth production. (© Bayreuther Festspiele)

The image of the artist as a lonely wanderer occurs freqently in Romantic art and literature. It can be seen, for example, in one of the most celebrated German paintings of the time, Caspar David Friedrich's *Monk by the Sea* (1809), where the artist has portrayed himself wandering alone sunk in contemplation, in an endless, featureless waste. 'It is delicious', wrote the author Kleist on seeing this picture in 1810, 'to experience an infinite solitude at the edge of the sea beneath a murky sky, to cast one's gaze out over a limitless waste of water. It is something else again to have made the voyage there and back, instead of which one wishes to pass over to the other side and cannot; one is stripped of everything necessary for life and yet perceives the voice of that life in the rumbling of the waves, the soughing of the air, the passage of clouds, the solitary cry of birds.

Heine introduces the Dutchman as 'the Wandering Jew of the ocean', a reference to another popular legend. Ahasuerus, like Vanderdecken, was doomed for blasphemy to ceaseless wandering, until the Day of Judgement. His crime was to have taunted Jesus on the way to Calvary. Coleridge merged the two legends in condemning his Mariner to wander both on land and sea; Goethe and Shelley were among later writers to be attracted by the theme. Halévy's grand opera *Le Juif errant* (1852) sets the legendary figure in a historical (medieval) context and concludes with a celestial vision of the Court of Heaven, before the Angel of Death orders the hapless Jew to continue — *'Marche! Marche toujours!'* Indeed, the Wandering Jew continued to be used as a metaphor for the artist for a long time, often by surprising people, such as the French realist painter Gustav Courbet. His portrait of himself with a patron, *Bonjour Monsieur Courbet* (1854) is based upon a popular print of the Wandering Jew. But then Courbet, realist though he was, had an ego as big as that of any Romantic artist.

The isolation of the Dutchman, reinforced by that of the Wandering Jew, had strong personal associations for both Heine and Wagner. Not only were they both, as artists, metaphorical exiles. They were also literal exiles, Germans living in Paris. The very different characters of their exiles is reflected in their attitudes to the *Dutchman* theme. Heine had left Germany in 1831, finding the atmosphere uncongenial to his liberal sympathies, and there was little to encourage him to return. Indeed, his writings were branded in 1835 as politically subversive. Artistically, too, he had distanced himself, for he was one of those artists who were trying to free themselves from romantic attitudes that seemed outworn. He treated the dominant themes of the day with irony.

This sense of distancing and irony can be found in Heine's account of the Dutchman legend. He pretends that his narrator saw it performed as a play in Amsterdam. He embroiders the theme by adding the romantic notion of the Dutchman being redeemable through the faithful love of a woman. Then he makes light of it. 'The devil, fool that he is, doesn't believe in the faithfulness of women.' The whole play simply becomes a frame for the most fickle of encounters with a Dutch adventuress that his narrator comes across in the audience.

Salvation, for Heine, is not to be taken seriously. For Wagner it was a different matter. All irony is removed in his adaptation of Heine's narrative. He may have been an exile at the time, but he had every hope of being redeemed though the establishment of a brilliant career. Yet even in his vision of redemption Wagner is aware of the peculiar position of the artist. The Dutchman does not return to earthly existence. And Wagner the artist, in his moment of triumph, would not re-enter the bourgeois world.

In a sense, Wagner was reclaiming Heine's version of the legend for Romanticism. For while this tendency had all but run its course in literature, it was still a potent force in music. Indeed, Wagner could be seen as the culmination of the movement in Germany, a view that would accord well with the assertion by A.W. Schlegel and other Romantic theorists that music was the supreme art form. The seriousness with which Wagner viewed the story can be seen in the way that

'The Stages of Life' by Caspar David Friedrich (Leipsig, Museum der Bildenden Künste)

Barbara Kemp as Senta (Stuart-Liff Collection)

he handled its details. He is deeply aware of its folklore basis. It seems significant that he should have shown Senta in a dreamlike state when we first encounter her. She is musing before the Dutchman's portrait. The legendary enters her life, so to speak, through the state of dreaming. Nothing could have been more typical of the German Romantic attitude to folk tales. Like dreams, they were seen as a means of access to the dark, unconscious side of experience. The two were specifically linked by Novalis when he claimed, 'All folk tales are no more than dreams of that native world that is everywhere and nowhere'. He himself used the notion of the dream entering conscious life in his novel *Heinrich von Ofterdingen*, where the hero's dream of a mystical blue flower at the beginning of the book sets him off on a quest. Even more relevant for Wagner was the use of the dream world by E.T.A. Hoffmann, the author whose views on music he found so revealing. In the introduction to one of his most bizarre tales, *Die Elixiren des Teufels* (*The Devil's Elixirs*) Hoffmann asks, 'Could it be that that which we call dream and fancy is, in fact, the symbolic recognition of the secret thread that runs through our life?'. It was such a secret thread that Senta recognized when Vanderdecken appeared before her.

The culmination of the opera is the Dutchman's death, which is seen as a release and a fulfilment. Once again this was a central notion for German Romantic writers, particularly for Novalis, whose cycle of poems *Hymns to the Night* constitutes a celebration of death. Only beyond mortal existence is it possible for the spirit to be fully absorbed in the totality of the universe. The state that is only intimated in dreaming can be fully achieved in death.

Even in the original legend the Dutchman's goal was death. It was perhaps for this reason that his ship was sometimes envisaged as a death ship, as did Coleridge in *The Ancient Mariner*. For Wagner, this part of the legend does not appear to have been of central interest, although in his stage directions he emphasizes the eerie circumstances of the appearance of his spectral ship and crew. In Berlin, where Wagner submitted his opera, the standards of scene painting had been revolutionized by Karl Friedrich Schinkel, the great Prussian architect who had designed a stupendous set for Mozart's *Magic Flute* in 1816. Schinkel had encouraged many accomplished painters to enter this field, including the brilliant landscapist Karl Blechen, who designed sets for works by Hoffmann and Weber. In Dresden, where the *Flying Dutchman* was first performed, artists of high standard were also employed by the theatre. They included the celebrated painter of folk scenes and idyllic landscapes, Adrian Ludwig Richter. Such artists were well versed in the associative use of natural forms. Richter, Blechen and Schinkel, indeed, had all been deeply impressed by the symbolic landscapes of the greatest German painter of the age, Caspar David Friedrich. Friedrich himself never undertook scene painting, but his use of imagery suggests interests akin to those found in Wagner's directions. Loneliness and the longing for death can frequently be found in his work. He often used the image of a ship coming into harbour to suggest the approach of death: a remarkable instance is *The Stages of Life*, in which an old man is beckoned towards the shore where a ghostly ship awaits him, silhouetted against the evening sky. Friedrich probably knew about the traditional image of the ship of death since he came from a sea port in Pomerania, where the legend was well known.

The death of Wagner's Dutchman, however, is far removed from the visions of Friedrich. It is a *Liebestod*, a culmination of love in death. Audiences of today perhaps identify less with Senta's determined self-sacrifice than with the Dutchman's sense of alienation. Isolation is no longer the prerogative of the artist. For all his fascination with the eerie sounds of the storm and the sea, Wagner drew his deepest inspiration from the psychological roots of the myth. It is his insight into the human qualities of his characters in the story, as much as its fantastic element, which makes for such excellent theatre.

An unidentified early set for the second act. (Royal College of Music)

Maurice Renaud as the Dutchman (Stuart-Liff Collection)

Norman Bailey as the Dutchman and Harold Blackburn as Daland at Sadler's Wells. (photo: Houston Rogers)

Donald McIntyre and Rita Hunter in the Sadler's Wells production by Dennis Arundell. (photo: Donald Southern)

The Overture to 'The Flying Dutchman'

Richard Wagner
translated by Melanie Karpinski

The dreaded ship of the 'Flying Dutchman' flies on the wings of the storm [1, 2, 3]; it nears the coast and drops anchor, for it is here that its captain has been promised salvation [4]; we hear the piteous strains of this message of redemption, which sound like a mixture of prayer and complaint [5]. The doomed man listens to them sullenly, bereft of hope: tired and longing for death he steps onto dry land, whilst his exhausted crew, weary of life, brings the ship silently to rest. — How often has this unhappy man already been through this scene! How often has he steered his ship towards land, where once in seven years it is granted him to step ashore; how often has he hoped to find the end to his torment, and oh!—how often has he found his hopes dashed and returned to his frenzied wanderings across the seas! In order to force his destruction he deliberately fought against billow and storm, steering his ship into the raging abyss — yet here it was not consumed; riding the billows he steered it towards the rocks — yet here it was not dashed to pieces. All the terrible dangers of the sea which once he scorned in his lust for victorious adventure now laugh at him — they cannot harm him, for he is cursed to sail the seas forever, hunting for spoils which cannot thrill him, and never to find that which alone could redeem him!

A stately ship sweeps past him; he hears the joyful song of the sailors who are happy to be nearing home [10, 11]: he is consumed with anger at such merriment and, borne by the storm, he flashes past furiously, frightening and silencing the happy singers and putting the crew to flight [2, 7]. He cries out for salvation from the depths of his misery: in the lifeless desert of his lone existence only a wife can bring him release [4, 6, 9]! But where does his rescuer live? Where does a heart beat in sympathy for him? Where is the one who will not flee from him in horror and fear, like these cowardly men, who make the sign of the cross at his arrival? A glimmer of light then breaks through his darkness and pierces his tormented soul like lightning [12]. It dies away, and then re-kindles: the seaman keeps the lodestar firmly in sight and steers determinedly through storm and wave towards it. What draws him so powerfully is the look of a woman which is full of sublime sadness and heaven-sent sympathy, which forces its way through to him! A heart has opened its unending depths to the sufferings of the doomed man: it must sacrifice itself to him, it must break with compassion and destroy itself in order to put an end to his misery. The cursed man breaks down at the sight of this divine vision, as his ship is dashed to pieces and engulfed by the ocean. He then rises, transfigured, from the waves, led by her victorious, rescuing hand towards the dawning of sublimest love.

A scene from Harry Kupfer's 1976 Bayreuth production (Festspielleitung Bayreuth)

Remarks on Performing the Opera 'The Flying Dutchman'

Richard Wagner
translated by Melanie Karpinski

First of all, I must remind both the conductor and the producer of what I stressed so strongly with regard to the production of *Tannhäuser*: namely the closest unity between what happens in the orchestra and what happens on stage. The ships and the sea, especially, demand an enormous amount of attention from the producer: he will find all the necessary indications at the corresponding places of the pianoforte edition or full score. The first scene has to evoke the mood of the opera in such a way that it becomes possible for the audience to grasp the concept of the mysterious figure of the 'Flying Dutchman' themselves: therefore it must be handled with exceptional care and sympathy; the sea between the headlands must be seen to rage and foam as much as possible; the representation of the ship cannot be too naturalistic: little touches, such as the heaving of the ship when struck by an exceptionally strong wave (during the two verses the Steersman's song) must be very clearly portrayed. The constant subtle changes in lighting demand especial care; in order to render as effective as possible the nuances in weather in the First Act, the skilful use of painted gauzes to reach as far as centre stage is indispensible. However, since these remarks are not specially directed to the purely decorative aspect of the performance (for which I must refer to the scenery of the opera as produced at the Schauspielhaus in Berlin) I am content — as stated — to plead for exact observation of my scattered scenic indications, whilst leaving the way they are carried out to the inventive powers of the scene-painter and the stage technician.

I shall therefore simply concern myself with the performers, and among these, more particularly with the representative of the very difficult principal male role of the Dutchman. The real success of the whole opera depends on the skilful presentation of the title role: its exponent must succeed in arousing and sustaining the greatest pity, and he will be able to do so if he observes the following main characteristics in his performance. His outward appearance has been sufficiently described. His first entry is extremely ceremonious and solemn: his slowness and hesitance when stepping onto dry land form a stark contrast to the unnatural speed of his ship over the sea. During the deep trumpet notes (B-minor), at the very end of the introductory scene, he has stepped off the deck, along a plank lowered by one of the crew, to a shelf of rock on the shore: the first notes of the ritornello in the aria (the deep E-sharp of the basses) accompany the Dutchman's first step on shore; his rolling gait, which is peculiar to sailors who have spent a long time away at sea, is accompanied by a wave-like figure for the cellos and violas; with the first crotchet of the third bar he takes his second step, — still with folded arms and bowed head; the third and fourth steps coincide with the notes of the eighth and tenth bars.

From this point on, his movements will naturally follow his general delivery, yet the performer must, under no pretext, be led astray into striding violently around the stage but must rather maintain a certain awe-inspiring calm in his outward demeanour, even during his most passionate expression of inner anguish and despair — in this way he will achieve the most effective characterisation. His first phrases should be sung without the slightest emotion, as by one completely exhausted (almost in strict beat, like the whole of this recitative); even at the words, *'ha, stolzer Ozean'*, which are sung with bitter fury, he does not betray any passion, but merely half turns his head in the direction of the sea with an expression of terrible scorn.

During the ritornello, after '*doch ewig meine Qual*', he bows his head once more, as though in utter weariness and despair; he sings, *'euch, des Weltmeers Fluthen'*, in this position, staring blankly before him. I should not like to cramp the singer too much in what he does during the *allegro* (*'wie oft in Meeres tiefsten Grund'*), but he must adhere to my main directives, namely, that however deep the passion, and however agonised the anguish with which he instils the vocal line, he must retain the greatest outward composure: a simple arm or hand movement — not too sweeping — will suffice to emphasise the more dramatic moments. Even the words, *'Niemals der Tod, nirgends ein Grab!'*, which must be sung with the most powerful emphasis, belong more to the description of his sufferings than to a direct and real outburst of his despair: he only reaches this with what follows, for which the most energetic action must therefore be reserved. With the repetition of the words, *'diess der Verdammniss Schreckgebot!'*, he bows both his head and his body quite deeply, and he remains in this position during the first four bars of the postlude: with the tremolo of the violins (E-flat) at the fifth bar he raises his eyes towards heaven, whilst his body remains bent low; with the entry of the muffled roll of the kettle-drum at the ninth bar of the postlude he begins to shudder uncontrollably and clench his fists convulsively at his sides, his lips trembling as he finally begins the phrase: *'Dich frage ich'* (still staring fixedly towards heaven). The whole of this, almost direct, address to the *'Engel Gottes'*, for all the awesome expression with which it is to be sung, must still be delivered in the position just indicated (without any marked change beyond what the execution necessarily demands at certain places): we must see before us a 'fallen angel' himself, whose fearful torment drives him to proclaim his wrath against Eternal Justice. Finally, with the words '*Vergeb'ne Hoffnung*', however, the full force of his despair finds expression: he stands tall and straight in his fury, his eyes still staring towards Heaven, and with the utmost energy of grief he casts all *'futile hope'* behind: he no longer wants to hear of promised release, and, (with the entry of the kettle-drum and basses) he crumples together on the floor, as if destroyed. With the opening of the *allegro-ritornello*, his features revive with a new and terrible last hope, the hope of the World's destruction, in which he too would die. This closing *allegro* requires the most terrible energy, not only in the vocal phrasing, but also in his gestures, for everything here is unmasked passion. Yet the singer must take pains to make this whole section, despite its vehemence of phrasing, seem but a mere gathering of all his forces for the final crushing outbreak at the words, *'Ihr Welten! endet euren Lauf!'* where he must reach a sublime climax. After the closing words (*'ewige Vernichtung, nimm mich auf!'*), he remains standing up straight, almost like a statue, throughout the whole *fortissimo* of the postlude: only with the *piano*, during the muffled chorus from the ship's hold, does he gradually relax his attitude; his arms sink to his sides, exhausted, he lowers his head at the four bars '*espressivo*' for the first violins, and during the last eight bars of the postlude he walks unsteadily to the cliff-face at the side: he leans his back against it and remains long in this position, his arms folded across his chest.

I have dealt with this scene in such detail in order to show the way I would like to have the Dutchman portrayed, and what weight I place on the most careful matching of the action to the music. The performer should take great pains to portray the rest of his role similarly. Moreover, this aria is the most difficult of the whole role, because the audience's further understanding of the subject depends

Heinrich Knöte as Erik in 1908. (Covent Garden Archives) He was greatly admired at Covent Garden and the Met. for his lyric tenor, although he never sang at Bayreuth.

upon the success of this scene: if this monologue has touched and penetrated the sympathy of the hearer as it should do, then the further success of the whole work is for the most part ensured — whereas nothing that comes later could possibly make up for anything neglected here.

In the following scene with Daland, the Dutchman remains initially in his previous position. He only raises his head slightly while answering Daland's questions from aboard ship. When Daland approaches him, on land, the Dutchman also advances to about the middle of the stage, with stately calm. His whole demeanour here expresses quiet, peaceful dignity; the expression of his voice is calm and noble, without a hint of stronger accent: he reacts and speaks here as from the force of old habit: he has already experienced so many similar encounters and conversations; everything, even the apparently purposeful questions and answers are made only half-consciously; he reacts as if under the constraint of his position, to which he submits mechanically, and without interest, like one exhausted. Just as instinctively his old yearning for redemption re-kindles: after his terrible outburst of despair he now appears milder and softer, and he expresses his longing for peace with touching sadness. He throws out the question, *'hast Du eine Tochter?'*, still with apparent calm; Daland's enthusiastic answer: *'fürwahr, ein treues Kind'* suddenly re-awakens the old hope in him (so often proved to be futile): he cries out in almost frenzied haste: *'sie sei mein Weib!'* He is once more caught by the old longing and describes his fate in the most poignant manner (remaining outwardly calm) with the words, *'Ach, ohne Weib, ohne Kind bin ich'*. The glowing colours in which Daland now paints his daughter revive more keenly the Dutchman's old yearning for *'Erlösung durch eines Weibes Treue'*, and in the duet's closing *allegro* the battle between hope and despair rises to the height of passion, in which hope seems almost to prevail.

In his first appearance before Senta in the Second Act the Dutchman's outward demeanour once more expresses complete calm and dignity: all his passionate emotions have been firmly imprisoned within him. Throughout the lengthy first *fermata* he remains motionless beside the door; at the beginning of the drum solo he slowly advances down stage; with the eighth bar of this solo he stops (the two bars *accelerando* for the strings relate to the gestures of Daland, who still stands surprised at the door, awaiting Senta's welcome, and he impatiently invites it with a movement of his outstretched arms); during the next three bars for the drum the Dutchman advances as far downstage as possible, where he now remains motionless, his eyes fixed on Senta. (The recurrence of the figure for the strings relates to the emphatic repetition of Daland's gesture: at the *pizzicato* on the next *fermata* he ceases to beckon to her, and shakes his head in amazement; with the entry of the basses after the *fermata*, he himself approaches Senta.)

The postlude of Daland's aria must be played in full: during the first four bars Daland turns to leave without further ado; with the fifth and sixth bars he stops and turns round again; the following seven bars accompany his partly pleased, partly curious and expectant gestures as he observes now Senta, and now the Dutchman; during the subsequent two bars for the double-basses he goes as far as the door, shaking his head; with the resumption of the theme by the wind instruments he puts his head back round the door and once more withdraws it in vexation, closing the door behind him, so that he has completely disappeared by the entry of the F-sharp chord for the wind instruments. The remainder of the postlude, together with the *ritornello* of the following duet, is accompanied by complete immobility and utter silence on stage: Senta and the Dutchman are lost in rapt contemplation of each other, from opposite sides of the stage. (The performers need not fear that the situation will bore the audience: it is a matter of experience that this is precisely the moment which most powerfully engrosses the spectator and best prepares him for the following scene.)

The whole succeeding E-major section should be executed by the Dutchman with an outward appearance of total calm and dignity, however passionate and moving his words; his hands and arms alone may be used (but only sparingly) to emphasise his stronger emotions.

The Dutchman does not stir until the two bars of the drum solo, before the following E-minor tempo, when he approaches Senta: during the short *ritornello* he moves a few steps towards the middle of the stage with a certain self-consciousness and mournful courtesy. (I must here tell the conductor that experience has shown me that I was mistaken in marking the tempo *un poco meno sostenuto*: the long preceeding tempo, admittedly, is somewhat slow at the beginning — particularly in the Dutchman's first solo — but little by little it instinctively brightens towards the close, so that with the entry of the E-minor the pace must necessarily be somewhat restrained once more, in order to give at least the opening of this section the feeling of solemn calm it requires. The four bar phrase, in fact, must be expressed in such a hesitant fashion that the fourth bar is

The first Bayreuth cast — 1901 (Royal College of Music)

played in strict *ritenuto*: the same thing applies to the first phrase now sung by the Dutchman.) With the ninth and tenth bars, during the drum solo, the Dutchman takes one, then two steps towards Senta. With the eleventh and twelfth bars, however, the tempo must become somewhat brisker, so that the B-minor (*'du könntest dich'*) expresses the tempo I really meant — *moderato*, certainly, but not quite so dragging — which is to be maintained throughout this section. At the *più animato ('so unbedingt, wie')* the Dutchman betrays the deep impression Senta's first words have made on him: he must sing this passage with more visible emotion. However, Senta's passionate cry (*'o, welche Leiden! Könnt' ich Trost ihm bringen!'*) moves him to the quick: with amazed admiration he softly stammers the words, *'welch' holder Klang im nächtlichen Gewühl?'*. With the *molto più animato* he is scarcely master of himself; he sings with the utmost fire of passion, and with the words, *'Allmächtiger, durch diese sei's!'*, he throws himself to his knees. With the *agitato* (B-minor) he rises to his feet impetuously: his love for Senta expresses itself in his terror at the thought of the danger she places herself in by reaching out the hand of salvation to him. He sees it as a hideous crime and in his passionate protest against her sharing in his fate he becomes a human being through and through, whereas up until now he has only given us the terrible impression of a ghost. Therefore the performer must give even his outer bearing the expression of human passion: he falls to the ground before Senta with the closing words: *'nennst ew'ge Treue du nicht dein!'* as if destroyed, so that Senta stands above him like an angel, as she tells him what she means by eternal loyalty. During the *ritornello* of the succeeding *allegro molto* the Dutchman raises himself with solemn exaltation: his voice rises to the sublimest heights of victory. In all that follows there can be no more room for misunderstanding: at his last entry, in the Third Act, all is passion, anguish, despair. I would especially stress that the singer should not drag the recitative passages but should take everything in the most spirited, forceful tempo.

Senta's role will be hard to misinterpret: I should just like to warn against one thing: the dreamy side of her nature must not be portrayed in a modern, sickly, sentimental fashion! In fact Senta is quite the opposite of this — she is a tough, Nordic girl, and even in her apparent sentimentality she is thoroughly naïve. Yet it is precisely such a naïve nature which, bred in that characteristically Nordic world, would be most susceptible to impressions, such as that of the ballad of the 'Flying Dutchman' and the picture of the pale sailor, and most inclined to succumb to the desire to redeem the damned: this takes the form of a powerful monomania in her, which is sometimes to be found in extremely naïve natures. It has been noted that Norwegian girls can be moved by such strong emotions that death is caused by the sudden stopping of the heart. Such a 'sickness' is also to be ascribed to the pale Senta.

Nor is Erik to be portrayed as a sentimental whiner: on the contrary he is stormy, impulsive and sombre, like every man who lives alone (particularly in the Northern Highlands). His cavatine in the Third Act should not be rendered in a sickly manner, which would do the role a gross injustice, but must, on the contrary, breathe heart-ache and melancholy. (Everything that might justify a false conception of this piece, such as its falsetto passage and final cadenza, I implore may be either altered or struck out.)

Furthermore I entreat the performer of Daland not to drag his role into the realm of comedy: he is a rough and hardy character drawn from life, a sailor who braves storms and dangers in the hope of gain and who in no way regards the sale (for so it must seem) of his daughter to a rich man as disgraceful: he thinks and acts like millions of others, without the least suspicion that he is doing any wrong.

Thematic Guide

Many of the themes from the opera have been identified in the articles by numbers in square brackets, which refer to the themes set out on these pages. The themes are also identified by the numbers in brackets at the corresponding points in the libretto, so that the words can be related to the musical themes.

OVERTURE *All examples in* 6/4

[1]

[2]

[3]

[4]

[5a]

[5b]

[6]

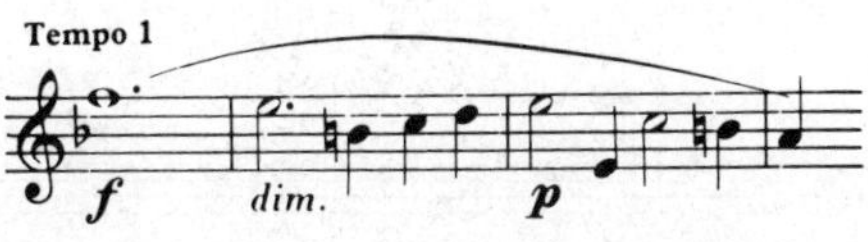

[7]

[8]

[9]

[10]

[11]

[12]

[13] **SAILORS**

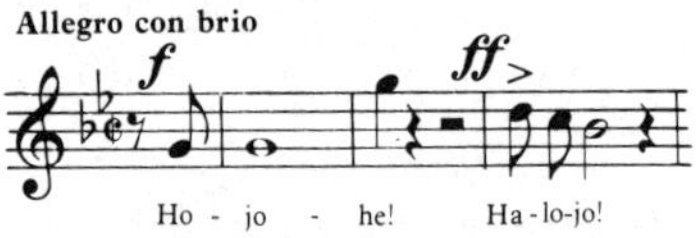

[14] **SAILORS**

[15]

[16] **DALAND**

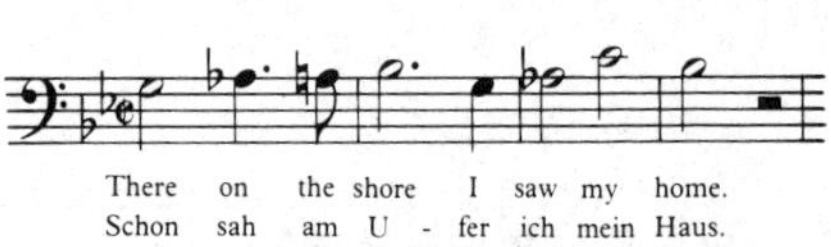

[17]

[18] **STEERSMAN**

[19] STEERSMAN

Moderato

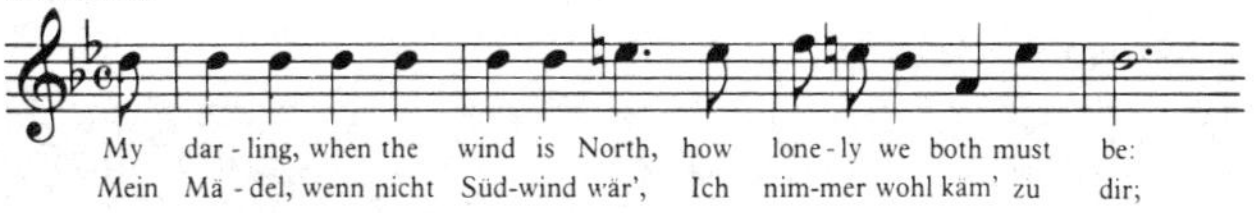

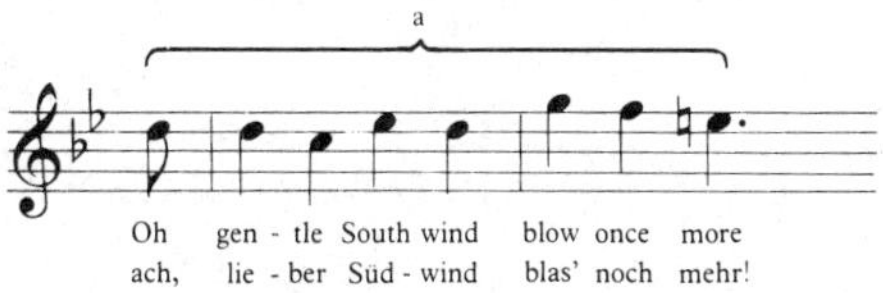

[20]

[21]

Allegro molto agitato

[22] DUTCHMAN

Maestoso

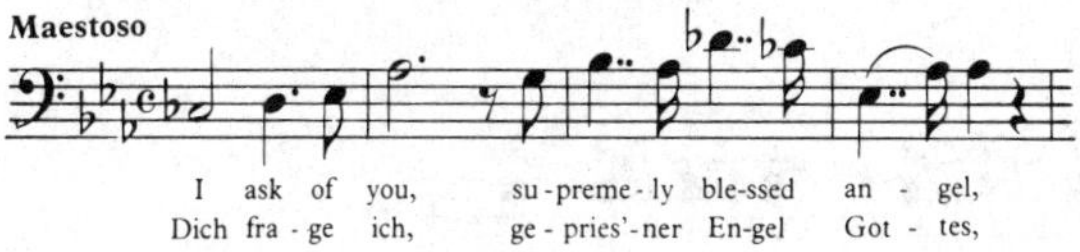

[23]

Molto passionato

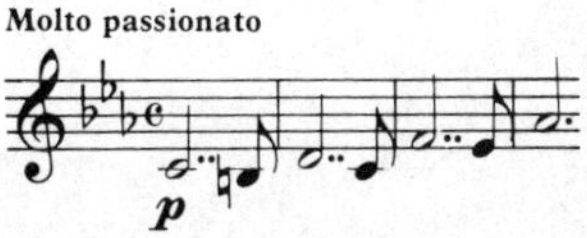

[24]

Lento

[25]

Animato

[26] GIRLS

Allegretto

[27a] SENTA

Allegro non troppo

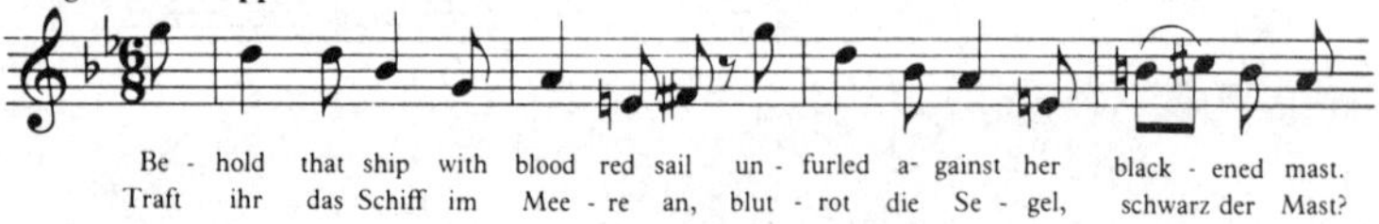

[27b]

[28] MARY

Prestissimo possibile

[29] ERIK

Allegro appassionato, ma un poco riten.

[30]

[31]

[32] *Aria No. 6*

Allegro moderato

[33] SENTA

Allegro molto

[34] *Trio*

Allegro vivace

[35] *The Norwegian Sailors' Dance* (*Compare* [17])

[Animato, ma non troppo Allegro]

[36]

[37]

[38] *No. 8 Finale*

[39]

[40] ERIK *Cavatine*

Andante

The Norwegian sailors sight their home port in the 1982 ENO production, designed by Stefanos Lazaridis. (photo: Reg Wilson)

The arrival of the Dutchman's ship in the ENON/Opera North production designed by Robin Don. (photo: Robin Don)

Der fliegende Holländer
The Flying Dutchman

Romantic Opera in Three Acts

Poem and Music by Richard Wagner

English Translation by David Pountney

The opera was first performed in Dresden on January 2, 1843. As *L'Olandese dannato* it was given in Italian, the first Wagner opera to reach England, at Drury Lane on July 23, 1870. Again in Italian, the American première was at the Philadelphia Academy of Music on November 8, 1876.

This translation was made for the 1982 English National Opera production by the producer David Pountney. Wagner's own stage directions have been translated especially for this edition and form no part of David Pountney's English text or production.

The German text follows Wagner's layout as closely as possible. Where alternative words or spellings between the printed poem and the vocal score appeared, the final version – the one actually set to music – has been adopted. Because the German lines do not begin with capital letters, the English has also been printed in this way, even in the verse songs, which it would have been misleading to set apart from the rest.

The numbers in square brackets refer to the Thematic Guide.

CHARACTERS

The Steersman	*tenor*
Daland *a Norwegian sea captain*	*bass*
The Dutchman	*baritone*
Senta *Daland's daughter*	*soprano*
Mary *Daland's house-keeper*	*mezzo-soprano*
Eric *a hunter*	*tenor*

Men and Women of the Village,
the Crews of the Dutchman's and of Daland's ship.

Act One

A steep cliff. The greater part of the stage is taken up by a wide expanse of sea. Terrible weather with a violent storm. Daland's ship has just cast anchor close to the shore; the sailors are calling to each other at their work of furling the sails, throwing out the ropes etc.. Daland has gone ashore. He is climbing the cliffs in an effort to reconnoitre the surrounding country. / No. 1 Introduction.

SAILORS

(*at work*) [10, 13, 14]

Hohoje! Hohoje! Halloho! Ho!	Hohoje! Hohoje! Halloho! Ho!

DALAND

(*climbing down from the cliff*)

I knew it! Seven miles from home, this blinding storm has swept us on. So near our long awaited goal, Fate has reserved one final blow!	Kein Zweifel! Sieben Meilen fort trieb uns der Sturm vom sich'ren Port. So nah' dem Ziel nach langer Fahrt, war mir der Streich noch aufgespart!

STEERSMAN

(*shouting through his cupped hands from the ship*)

Ho! Are you there?	[2] Ho! Kapitän!

DALAND

How is the ship? Secure?	Am Bord bei euch, wie steht's?

STEERSMAN

Yes, she is safe. The anchor's holding fast.	Gut, Kapitän! Wir sind auf sich'rem Grund!

DALAND

It's Sandwike; I know the bay of old. —	[15] Sandwike ist's! Genau kenn' ich die Bucht. —
What luck! There on the shore I saw my home, Senta, my child, I felt my arms around you: — One gust of wind has blasted us away . . . Trust in the wind and the Devil confounds you!	[16] Verwünscht! Schon sah am Ufer ich mein Haus, Senta, mein Kind, glaubt' ich schon zu umarmen: — Da bläst es aus dem Teufelsloch heraus . . . Wer baut auf Wind, baut auf Satan's Erbarmen!

(*going on board*)

Ah well, be calm. The storm will pass, such furious weather cannot last. —	Was hilft's? Geduld, der Sturm lässt nach, wenn so er tobt, dann währt's nicht lang. —
All right men! You deserve your rest . . . To bed with you! Danger is past!	He, Bursche! Lange war't ihr wach, zur Ruhe denn! Mir ist's nicht bang!

(*The sailors go below decks.*)

Keep watch for me, I'll go below and get some sleep. There's nought to fear but better to be sure.	Nun, Steuermann, die Wache nimmst du wohl für mich? Gefahr ist nicht, doch gut ist's, wenn du wachst.

STEERSMAN

I'll keep the watch. Sleep soundly, all is well!	Seid ausser Sorg'! Schlaft ruhig, Kapitän!

Daland goes into his cabin. The steersman is alone on deck. The storm has eased somewhat but still rises again from time to time. A heavy swell is running out at sea. [17] *The steersman has one last look round, then sits down by the wheel. He yawns. He shakes himself awake. / Song.*

I

In the teeth of the storm across the seas — [18]	Mit Gewitter und Sturm aus fernem Meer —
my darling, I am near!	mein Mädel, bin dir nah!
Over towering waves the Southern breeze —	Über turmhohe Flut von Süden her —
my darling, brought me here!	mein Mädel, ich bin da!
My darling, when the wind is North, [19]	Mein Mädel, wenn nicht Südwind wär',
how lonely we both must be:	ich nimmer wohl käm' zu dir:
Oh gentle South wind, blow once more! [19b]	Ach, lieber Südwind, blas' noch mehr!
My darling is calling me.	Mein Mädel verlangt nach mir.

A large wave rocks the ship. The steersman gets up to see if any damage has been done, then satisfied, settles down again. [17, 14]

II

As I walked on a lonely Southern sand —	Von des Südens Gestad', aus weitem Land —
I stopped and thought of you;	ich hab' an dich gedacht;
through the storms of that distant Moorish land	durch Gewitter und Meer vom Mohrenstrand
a gift I brought for you.	hab' dir 'was mitgebracht.
My darling, may that wind not fail,	Mein Mädel, preis' den Südwind hoch,
I've brought you a golden ring.	ich bring' dir ein gülden Band.
Oh gentle South wind, fill our sail!	Ach, lieber Südwind, blase doch!
I'll marry my darling.	Mein Mädel hätt' gern den Tand.

He struggles against his exhaustion but finally falls asleep. The sea is once more restless. It grows darker and the storm picks up again. In the distance the Flying Dutchman's ship appears with blood-red sails and black masts. It quickly approaches the coast and rides alongside the Norwegian vessel. [1] *The anchor drops with a terrifying crash. The steersman gets up and looks at the wheel; convinced that nothing has happened he sits down again and hums the start of his song. He falls asleeep again. Without the slightest sound the ghostly crew of the Dutchman's berth their ship. The Dutchman in black Spanish costume comes on land.** [1, 14, 3, 19, 17] / *No. 2 Aria* [20]

DUTCHMAN

The term is up. Once more the seven years	Die Frist ist um, und abermals verstrichen
have run their course. — The jaded sea casts me	sind sieben Jahr'. — Voll Überdruss wirft mich
upon the shore . . . Ha, curb your arrogance!	das Meer an's Land . . . Ha, stolzer Ozean!
It won't be long before once more you bear me!	In kurzer Frist sollst du mich wieder tragen!
Your threat may waver, my pain can never end! —	Dein Trotz ist beugsam, — doch ewig meine Qual! —
Once more I come to seek salvation,	Das Heil, das auf dem Land' ich suche,
but I shall not find it! — You eternal ocean	nie werd' ich es finden! — Euch, des Weltmeer's Fluten,
I am your slave, until the final breaker	bleib' ich getreu, bis eure letzte Welle
is still, and every drop has drained away! —	sich bricht, und euer letztes Nass versiegt! —
— I sought the ocean's dark abyss [21]	— Wie oft in Meeres tiefsten Schlund
trying so desperately to drown: —	stürzt ich voll Sehnsucht mich hinab: —
but no, my death, it was not there! [6]	doch ach! den Tod, ich fand ihn nicht!
And where the currents roar and hiss,	Da, wo der Schiffe furchtbar Grab,
I drove my helpless ship aground: —	trieb mein Schiff ich zum Klippengrund: —
but no, my grave, it was not there! —	doch ach! mein Grab, es schloss sich nicht! —
I dared the pirates to do battle,	Verhöhnend droht' ich dem Piraten,
in violent death I sought relief:	im wilden Kampfe hofft' ich Tod:
"Hear my challenge! Come and show your mettle!	"Hier" — rief ich — "zeige deine Thaten!
The ship is rich beyond belief!" — [1]	Von Schätzen voll ist Schiff und Boot." —

* Wagner's detailed description of the following scene may be found on page 37.

But no, the brutes begin to pray. They cross themselves and slink away. — Nowhere to lie! Never to die! This is damnation's dread decree. — —	Doch ach! des Meer's barbar'scher Sohn schlägt bang das Kreuz und flieht davon.— Nirgends ein Grab! Niemals der Tod! Dies der Verdammnis Schreckgebot. — —
I ask of you, supremely blessed angel, you who revealed my vision of release: was I your plaything, mocked and then deluded, when you awoke my only hope of peace? —	[22] Dich frage ich, gepries'ner Engel Gottes, der meines Heils Bedingung mir gewann: war ich Unsel'ger Spielwerk deines Spottes, als die Erlösung du mir zeigtest an? —
To hope is futile! Vain to dream of death!	[20] Vergeb'ne Hoffnung! Furchtbar eitler Wahn!
Eternal love has vanished — from the earth!	Um ew'ge Treu' auf Erden — ist's gethan? — —
	[23]
A single ray of hope consoles me, a single firm belief remains: the earth that puts forth growth and blossoms, must also turn to dust again . . . Day of Judgement! Glorious day! When will that dawn break through to me? You, herald, bid the trumpet play! Announce the world's catastrophe!	Nur eine Hoffnung soll mir bleiben, nur eine unerschüttert steh'n: so lang' der Erde Keime treiben — so muss sie doch zu Grunde geh'n . . . Tag des Gerichtes! Jüngster Tag! Wann brichst du an in meine Nacht? Wann dröhnt er, der Vernichtungs-Schlag, mit dem die Welt zusammenkracht?
And at the rising of the dead, the void will close about my head . . . You planets, you have run your course! Endless oblivion I am yours!	[23] Wann alle Toten aufersteh'n, dann werde ich in Nichts vergeh'n . . . Ihr Welten, endet euren Lauf! Ew'ge Vernichtung, nimm mich auf!

[1]

CHORUS

(*from the Dutchman's crew below decks*)

Endless oblivion we are yours!	Ew'ge Vernichtung, nimm uns auf!

(*The Dutchman, with his head bowed, and arms crossed on his chest, leans on the cliff-face downstage. He remains motionless in this position.*) [1]

No. 3. Scene: Duet and Chorus

DALAND

(*He comes out of the cabin and notices the strange ship.* [17] *He looks round for the steersman.*)

Hey steersman! Stir yourself!	He! Holla! Steuermann!

STEERSMAN

(*raising himself sleepily*)

All clear, all clear.	's ist nichts! 's ist nichts.
Ah, gentle South wind, blow once more, my darling . . .	[19b] Ach, lieber Südwind, blas' noch mehr, mein Mädel . . .

DALAND

(*shaking the steersman*)

Can't you see? Well, you call that keeping watch? There is a ship . . . were you so sound asleep?	Du siehst nichts? Gelt, du wachest brav, mein Dursch, dort liegt ein Schiff . . . wie lange schlief'st du schon?

STEERSMAN

(*getting up rapidly*)

My God I was! Forgive me, I was tired!	Zum Teufel auch! Verzeiht mir, Kapitän! —

(*He quickly takes a loud hailer and calls out*)

Hello!	Wer da?

(*long pause and echoes are heard*)

Hello!	Wer da?

DALAND

It seems they are as fast asleep as us.	Es scheint sie sind gerad' so faul als wir.

STEERSMAN

Give answer! Name and country!	Gebt Antwort! Schiff und Flagge?

DALAND

(*who gestures as he notices the Dutchman on land*)

Ah wait! I think that must be the captain. —	Lass' ab! Mich dünkt, ich seh' den Kapitän. —
Hey! Hello! Captain! What ship are you? Your country?	He! Holla! Seemann! Nenne dich! Wess' Landes?

(*long pause*) [24]

DUTCHMAN

(*He does not change his position but slightly moves his head.*)

I've travelled far: in storm I sought an	Weit komm' ich her; verwehrt bei Sturm und
anchorage — would you refuse it me?	Wetter ihr mir den Ankerplatz?

DALAND

Good heavens no! Hospitality is our custom.	Behüt' es Gott! Gastfreundschaft kennt der Seemann.

(*going ashore*)

Who are you?	Wer bist du?

DUTCHMAN

A Dutchman.	Holländer.

DALAND

God be with you! So you were also driven to this God-forsaken bay?	Gott zum Gruss! So trieb auch dich der Sturm an diesen nackten Felsenstrand?
I fared no better: just a mile or so from home and all my family, almost there, and then I could not make a landing.	Mir ging's nicht besser: wenig Meilen nur von hier ist meine Heimat; fast erreicht, musst' ich auf's neu' mich von ihr wenden.
Where have you come from? Have you suffered any damage?	Sag', woher kommst du? Hast Schaden du genommen?

(*He inspects the Dutch ship.*)

DUTCHMAN

My ship is sound, it seems it can't be damaged. [24]	Mein Schiff ist fest, es leidet keinen Schaden.
The storm and wind cannot appal me,	Durch Sturm und bösen Wind verschlagen,
I must go on not knowing why, —	irr' auf den Wassern ich umher, —
my journeys, I cannot recall them:	wie lange? weiss ich kaum zu sagen:
year after year just passes by.	schon zähl'ich nicht die Jahre mehr.
I can't imagine or remember	Unmöglich dünkt mich's, dass ich nenne
the many lands that I have known:	die Länder alle, die ich fand:
the only one I seek forever —	das Eine nur, nach dem ich brenne —
cannot be found, my final home! —	ich find' es nicht, mein Heimatland! —
Oblige me then and let me be your guest. [24]	Vergönne mir auf kurze Frist dein Haus
You won't regret the day you were my friend.	und deine Freundschaft soll dich nicht gereu'n:
My ship is fully loaded with a cargo of precious stones and jewels: if you wish to,	mit Schätzen aller Gegenden und Zonen ist reich mein Schiff beladen: willst du handeln
you have the chance to make a handsome profit.	so sollst du sicher deines Vorteils sein.

DALAND

The tale is strange. Should I believe your story?	Wie wunderbar! Soll deinem Wort ich glauben?
An evil star has dogged your steps till now.	Ein Unstern, scheint's, hat dich bis jetzt verfolgt.

If I can help you, I'll do all I can.
But tell me further
what your ship contains.

Um dir zu frommen, biet' ich, was ich kann:
doch — darf ich fragen,
was dein Schiff enthält?

(*At a sign from the Dutchman two of his crew bring a large box ashore.*)

DUTCHMAN

It carries all the rarest jewels on earth,
rubies and diamonds, precious stones and pearls.
Look in, then you can calculate how much
I am offering, if I were to be your guest this evening.

Die seltensten der Schätze sollst du seh'n,
kostbare Perlen, edelstes Gestein.
Blick' hin, und überzeuge dich vom Werte
des Preises, den ich für ein gastlich Dach dir biete!

DALAND
(*looking at the contents of the box in astonishment*)

What? Can you mean it? All these jewels?
Who could afford the price of so much treasure?

Wie? Ist's möglich? Diese Schätze!
Wer ist so reich, den Preis dafür zu bieten?

DUTCHMAN

The price? It is exactly as I said:
this is the payment for a single night!
But what you see is just the smallest part
of all that's lying hidden in the hold.
What use is gold? I have neither wife
nor child, and I shall never find my home!
I gladly offer all my wealth, if you
would only let me make my home with you.

Den Preis? So eben hab' ich ihn genannt:
dies für das Obdach einer einz'gen Nacht!
Doch, was du siehst, ist nur der kleinste Teil
von dem, was meines Schiffes Raum verschliesst.
[24] Was frommt der Schatz? Ich habe weder Weib,
noch Kind, und meine Heimat find' ich nie!
All' meinen Reichtum biet' ich dir, wenn bei
den Deinen du mir neue Heimat giebst.

DALAND

I am bewildered.

Was muss ich hören?

DUTCHMAN

Do you have a daughter?

Hast du eine Tochter?

DALAND

I do, a lovely girl.

Fürwahr, ein treues Kind.

DUTCHMAN

Let her be my wife!

Sie sei mein Weib!

DALAND
(*disconcerted but delighted*)

What? Be his wife! He would marry my child?
I really did hear him say it! . . .
I must decide or he might change his mind,
I dare not even delay it.
Surely, he's the man she should marry!
Could all this be a marvellous dream?
A fool would ignore such good fortune!
I shall very gladly agree, very gladly.

Wie? Hör' ich recht? Meine Tochter sein Weib?
Er selbst spricht aus den Gedanken!
Fast fürcht' ich, wenn unentschlossen ich bleib',
müsst' er im Vorsatze wanken.
Wüsst' ich, ob ich wach' oder träume!
Kann ein Eidam willkommener sein?
Ein Thor, wenn das Glück ich versäume!
Voll Entzücken schlage ich ein.

DUTCHMAN

I am alone with no wife or child,
all ties of love are denied me!
Only the restless pursuit of fate

Ach, ohne Weib, ohne Kind bin ich,
mich fesselt nichts an die Erde!
Rastlos verfolgte das Schicksal mich,

whose hatred is always beside me.
My home is the wind and the water:
my wealth can bring no joy any more,
but if I could marry your daughter,
oh, then all I possess would be yours!

die Qual nur war mir Gefährte.
Nie werd' ich die Heimat erreichen:
zu was frommt mir der Güter Gewinn?
Lässt du zu dem Bund dich erweichen,
O, so nimm meine Schätze dahin!

DALAND

[25]

Yes, stranger, I possess a lovely daughter.
Her childish heart is full of love for me.
She is my pride, the best of my possessions,
she soothes my troubles and inspires my joy.

Wohl, Fremdling, hab' ich eine schöne Tochter,
mit treuer Kindeslieb' ergeben mir;
sie ist mein Stoltz, das höchste meiner Güter,
mein Trost im Unglück, meine Freud' im Glück.

DUTCHMAN

And may she never cease to love her father,
true love may she then give her husband too.

Dem Vater stets bewahr' sie ihre Liebe,
ihm treu, wird sie auch treu dem Gatten sein.

DALAND

You offer jewels, priceless pearls and diamonds
but I am offering more: a faithful wife —

Du giebst Jewelen, unschätzbare Perlen,
das höchste Kleinod doch, ein treues Weib —

DUTCHMAN

Then you agree?

Du giebst sie mir?

DALAND

I give you my consent.
Your story moved me; you are a generous man,
and that to me denotes a noble mind:
her bridegroom should be so, and if your wealth
were half so much, I would not choose another.

Ich gebe dir mein Wort.
Michrührt dein Loos; freigebig, wie du bist,
zeigst Edelmut und hohen Sinn du mir:
den Eidam wünscht' ich so, und wär' dein Gut
auch nicht so reich, wählt' ich doch keinen And'ren.

DUTCHMAN

My friend! May I see the girl today?

Hab' Dank! Werd' ich die Tochter heut' noch seh'n?

DALAND

The next fair wind shall bring us to my house;
then you shall see her and if you like her well —

Der nächste günst'ge Wind führt uns nach Haus;
du sollst sie seh'n, und wenn sie der gefällt —

DUTCHMAN

She'll be my wife . . .

So ist sie mein . . .

(*to himself*)

Will she redeem my life?
If I should crave my soul's salvation
from black despair and mortal pain,
am I allowed this aspiration
the only hope that can remain?
May I still, though all in vain, remember,
once there was an angel sweet and kind?
The darkness, could it now surrender,
and free my poor tormented mind?
Ah! All is hopeless, that I know,
yet hope revives and longs to grow!

Wird sie mein Engel sein? —
Wenn aus der Qualen Schreckgewalten
die Sehnsucht nach dem Heil mich treibt,
ist mir's erlaubt, mich festzuhalten
an einer Hoffnung, die mir bleibt?
Darf ich in jenem Wahn noch schmachten,
dass sich ein Engel mir erweicht?
Der Qualen, die mein Haupt umnachten,
ersehntes Ziel hätt' ich erreicht?
Ach! Ohne Hoffnung, wie ich bin,
geb' ich der Hoffnung doch mich hin!

DALAND

Salute the mighty power of the ocean
which drove me here to meet this man!
I simply have to keep possession
of what by luck has come to hand.
The wind that brought us both together,
be thanked, though you are harsh and wild!
What is the aim of every father?
A wealthy husband for his child.
A man with such an honest soul
can take my daughter and my home!

Gepreisen seid, des Sturms Gewalten,
die ihr an diesen Strand mich triebt!
Fürwahr, blos brauch' ich fest zu halten,
was sich so schön von selbst mir giebt.
Die ihn an diese Küste brachten,
ihr Winde, sollt gesegnet sein!
Ja, wonach alle Väter trachten,
ein reicher Eidam, er ist mein.
Dem Mann mit Gut und hohem Sinn
geb froh ich Haus und Tochter hin!

STEERSMAN
(on board)

South wind! South wind!
"Oh, gentle South wind, blow once more!"

Südwind! Südwind!
[19a] "Ach, lieber Südwind, blas' noch mehr!"

SAILORS

Hohohe! Halloho!

[13] Hohohe! Halloho!

DALAND

Today your fortune cannot fail:
the wind is fair, the sea is calm.
Raise the anchor and set sail
and very soon we shall be home.

[17] Du siehst, das Glück ist günstig dir:
der Wind ist gut, die See in Ruh.
Sogleich die Anker lichten wir
und segeln schnell der Heimat zu.

DUTCHMAN

You would oblige me if you sailed on ahead;
the wind is fresh but I must rest my men;
for after such a storm they'll rest instead.

[14] Darf ich bitten, segelst du voran;
[7] der Wind ist frisch, doch meine Mannschaft müd';
ich gönn ihr kurze Ruh' und folge dann.

DALAND

But our wind?

Doch, unser Wind?

DUTCHMAN

It will not change again!
My ship is swift, we shan't be far behind.

Er bläst noch lang' aus Süd!
Mein Schiff ist schnell, es holt dich sicher ein.

DALAND

I see. Alright, if you've made up your mind!
Farewell, let's hope you'll see my child today!

Du glaubst? Wohlan, es möge denn so sein!
Leb' wohl, mögst heute du mein Kind noch seh'n!

DUTCHMAN

Indeed!

Gewiss!

DALAND
(going on board his ship)

Hey! How the wind has filled the sails!
Hallo! Hallo! Quick, let us set to work!

Hei! Wie die Segel schon sich bläh'n!
Hallo! Hallo! Frisch, Jungen, greifet an!

(There is a blast on the ship's whistle.)

SAILORS
(setting sail jubilantly)

In the teeth of the storm across the seas —
my darling, I am near!
Over towering waves the Southern breeze,
my darling, brought me here!

[18] Mit Gewitter und Sturm aus fernem Meer —
mein Mädel, bin dir nah'!
Über turmhohe Flut vom Süden her —
mein Mädel, ich bin da!

My darling, when the wind is North,	[19] Mein Mädel, wenn nicht Südwind wär',
how lonely we both must be;	ich nimmer wohl käm' zu dir;
Ah, gentle South wind, blow once more,	ach, lieber Südwind, blas' noch mehr!
my darling is calling me.	Mein Mädel verlangt nach mir.

The Dutchman boards his ship. The curtain falls. [17, 2, 3, 14]

Herbert Janssen as the Dutchman (Met. Archives)

David Ward as the Dutchman, a role he first sang in Dennis Arundell's famous production at Sadler's Wells in 1959, at Covent Garden in 1966. (photo: Reg Wilson)

Act Two

A large room in Daland's house with nautical objects on the wall, such as maps etc.. On the back wall there is a picture of a pale man with a dark beard, wearing a black, Spanish costume. Mary and the girls are sitting round the fire, spinning. Senta, leaning back in a large armchair, is sunk in contemplation of the picture on the wall. / No. 4. Scene: Song and Ballad.

CHORUS OF GIRLS

Hum and thrum as you are spinning, [26]
spin until the work is done!
Spin until the wool is thinning,
busy wheel go hum and thrum!
My darling far away at sea,
just think of me
where'er you roam;
my little wheel spin fast and free!
If you could blow,
he'd soon come home!

Summ' und brumm' du gutes Rädchen,
munter, munter dreh' dich um!
Spinne, spinne tausend Fädchen,
gutes Rädchen, brumm' und summ'!
Mein Schatz ist auf dem Meere draus,
er denkt nach Haus
an's fromme Kind;
mein gutes Rädchen, braus' und saus'!
Ach! gäbst du Wind,
er käm' geschwind.

MARY

So busy, busy with your spinning,
but I know exactly what you're thinking.

Ei! Fleissig, fleissig! Wie sie spinnen!
Will jede sich den Schatz gewinnen.

GIRLS
(*with playful seriousness*)

Now Mary wait, full well you know,
there's still another verse to go!

Frau Mary, still! Denn wohl ihr wisst,
das Lied noch nicht zu Ende ist!

MARY

Well sing, it helps the wheel to spin. —
Senta, stop dreaming! Why not join in?

So singt! Dem Rädchen lässt's nicht Ruh. —
Du aber, Senta, schweigst dazu?

GIRLS

Hum and thrum as you are spinning,
spin until the work is done!
Spin until the wool is thinning,
busy wheel go hum and thrum!
My darling sails upon the sea,
and gathers fine
and precious things;
ah, little wheel spin fast and free —!
Perhaps he'll bring
a golden ring.
Neat and nimble! Spin the spindle!

Summ' und brumm' du gutes Rädchen,
munter, munter dreh' dich um!
Spinne, spinne tausend Fädchen,
gutes Rädchen, brumm' und summ'!
Mein Schatz da draussen auf dem Meer,
im Süden er
viel Gold gewinnt;
ach, gutes Rädchen, saus' noch mehr —!
Er giebt's dem Kind,
wenn's fleissig spinnt.
Fleissig, Mädchen! Gutes Rädchen!

MARY
(*to Senta*)

You lazy girl, if you won't spin,
you don't deserve one single thing.

Du böses Kind, wenn du nicht spinnst,
von Schatz du kein Geschenk gewinnst.

GIRLS

She's not like us, her time is free;
Her darling's not away at sea.
Instead of gold, he's after game!
These hunting folk are all the same!

Sie hat's nicht not, dass sie sich eilt;
ihr Schatz nicht auf dem Meere weilt.
Bringt er nicht Gold, bringt er doch Wild, —
man weiss ja, was ein Jäger gilt!

(*Senta sings softly to herself without changing her position.*) [5]

MARY

You see her gazing at that face! —	Da seht ihr's! immer vor dem Bild! —
How can you waste your youth and beauty	Wirst du dein ganzes junges Leben
with all this idle fantasy?	verträumen vor dem Konterfei?

SENTA
(*without changing her position*)

How could his story not have moved me,	Was hast du Kunde mir gegeben,
whoever suffered more than he?	was mir erzählet, wer er sei! —

(*sighing*)

Unhappy man!	Der arme Mann!

MARY

Now that's enough!	Gott sei mit dir!

GIRLS

Ei, ei! Ei, ei! What did she say?	Ei, ei! Ei, ei! was hören wir!
She's sighing. How it breaks her heart!	Sie seufzet um den bleichen Mann!
You see — beware the snares of art!	Da sieht man, was ein Bild doch kann!

MARY
(*losing patience*)

I'm sure the girl will go insane.	Den Kopf verliert sie noch darum.
It's useless, every day's the same.	Nichts hilft es, wenn ich täglich brumm'!
Come Senta, stop that silly game!	Komm' Senta! Wend' dich doch herum!

GIRLS

She's so in love, she's miles away.	Sie hört euch nicht, sie ist verliebt.
Ei, ei! What will poor Erik say?	Ei, ei! Wenn's nur nicht Händel giebt!
His blood is hot, his temper wild, —	Denn Erik har gar heisses Blut, —
to think he might attack the child!	dass er nur keinen Schaden thut!
Beware! He'll come to scare us all	Sagt nichts! — er schiesst sonst, Wut entbrannt,
and blast his rival off the wall.	den Nebenbuhler von der Wand.

SENTA
(*angrily*)

Enough! Stop all this stupid laughter	O schweigt! Mit eurem tollen Lachen
or else you'll really make me angry!	wollt ihr mich enstlich böse machen?

(*The girls sing as loudly as possible and spin their wheels with a great clatter so that Senta has no chance to scold them.*)

GIRLS

Hum and thrum as you are spinning,	[26] Summ' und brumm'! Du gutes Rädchen,
spin until the work is done!	munter, munter dreh' dich um!
Spin until the wool is thinning,	Spinne, spinne tausend Fädchen,
busy wheel, go hum and thrum!	gutes Rädchen, brumm' und summ'!

SENTA

Oh please excuse me if I mention	O, macht dem dummen Lied ein Ende,
your hum and thrum gets on my nerves!	es summt und brummt nur vor dem Ohr!
I'll very gladly pay attention,	Wollt ihr, dass ich mich zu euch wende,
if that is what the song deserves!	so sucht 'was Besseres hervor!

GIRLS

Good, sing yourself!	Gut, singe du!

SENTA

Mary will sing for me	Hört, was ich rate: —
and tell once more the Dutchman's story.	Frau Mary singst uns die Ballade.

MARY

Now God forbid! That would be wrong!	Bewahre Gott! das fehlte mir!
Please let the Dutchman rest in peace!	[1] Den fliegenden Holländer lasst in Ruh!

SENTA

You often used to sing the song!	Wie oft doch hört' ich sie von dir!
I'll sing it myself. Listen with care!	Ich sing' sie selbst, hört, Mädchen, zu!
Since to your hearts I am appealing,	Lasst mich's euch recht zum Herzen führen,
his fate should move your deepest feeling!	des Aermsten Loos, es muss euch rühren!

GIRLS

Yes, we agree.	Uns ist es recht.

SENTA

Mark every word!	Merkt auf die Wort'!

GIRLS

The wheels are still!	Dem Spinnrad Ruh!

MARY
(*annoyed*)

It's quite absurd!	Ich spinne fort!

(*The girls, after they have set their wheels aside, gather around Senta. Mary stays by the fire-place and continues to spin. Senta remains in the big armchair.*)

SENTA
Ballad
I [1]

Yohohoe! Yohohohoe!		Johohoe! Johohohoe!
Behold the ship with blood-red sail	[27]	Traft ihr das Schiff im Meere an,
unfurled against her blackened mast.		blutrot die Segel, schwarz der Mast?
There stands her master, gaunt and pale,		Auf hohem Bord der bleiche Mann,
who knows how long his watch must last?		des Schiffes Herr, wacht ohne Rast.
Hui! The north wind sighs! —	[3, 15]	Hui! Wie saust der Wind! —
Yohohoe!	[7]	Johohoe!
Hui! It shrieks and groans! —		Hui! Wie pfeift's im Tau! —
Yohohoe!		Johohoe!
Hui! Like an arrow he flies,		Hui! Wie ein Pfeil fliegt er hin,
without rest, without aim, without hope! —	[4]	ohne Ziel, ohne Rast, ohne Ruh! —
One chance remains to gain this poor man his peace and salvation,	[5]	Doch kann dem bleichen Manne Erlösung einstens noch werden,
only a woman true unto death can bring him redemption! —		fänd er ein Weib, das bis in den Tod getreu ihm auf Erden!
Ah, haunted man, who can tell when you'll find her?		Ach! Wann wirst du, bleicher Seemann, sie finden?
May God in Heaven grant you		Betet zum Himmel, dass bald
a wife faithful and true!		ein Weib Treue ihm halt'!

(*Towards the end of the verse Senta approaches the picture. The girls listen sympathetically. Mary has stopped spinning.*)

II [1]

The storm wind blew with bitter force	[27]	Bei bösem Wind und Sturmes Wut
as once he fought the rising sea.		umsegelen wollt' er einst ein Kap: —
He shouted then that reckless curse:		er flucht' und schwur mit tollem Mut:
"I'll fight you till eternity!" —		"in Ewigkeit lass' ich nicht ab!" —
Hui! And Satan heard, —	[3, 15]	Hui! Und Satan hört's —
Yohohoe!	[7]	Johohoe!
Hui! And took his word —		Hui! Nahm ihn bei'm Wort! —
Yohohoe!		Johohoe!
Hui! So condemned he must sail		Hui! Und verdammt zieht er nun
on and on, without rest, without hope! —	[4]	durch das Meer ohne Rast, ohne Ruh! —

One chance remains to gain this poor man his peace and salvation, [5]
only a woman true unto death can bring him redemption.
Ah, wretched man, who can tell when you'll find her!
May God in Heaven grant you
a wife faithful and true!

Doch, dass der arme Mann noch Erlösung fände auf Erden,
zeigt' Gottes Engel an, wie sein Heil ihm einst könne werden:
Ach! Könntest du, bleicher Seemann, es finden!
Betet zum Himmel, das bald
ein Weib Treue ihm halt'!

(*Senta, who had already risen for the second verse, steps forward with growing excitement.*)

III [1]

Each seven years he lands again, [27]
to seek that true and faithful bride: —
each seven years he seeks again,
but sails alone upon the tide. —
Hui! "So hoist the sail!" — [3, 17]
Yohohoe!
Hui! "Cast off the boat!" —
Yohohoe!
Hui! "Love is false, so is faith!
To the sea, without rest, without hope!" —

Vor Anker alle sieben Jahr,
ein Weib zu frei'n, geht er an's Land: —
er freite alle sieben Jahr',
noch nie ein treues Weib er fand. —
Hui! "Die Segel auf!" —
Johohoe!
Hui! "Den Anker los!" —
Johohoe!
Hui! "Falsche Lieb', falsche Treu'!
Auf, in See, ohne Rast, ohne Ruh!" —

[4]

(*Senta is so deeply affected that she sinks back into the chair. The girls, also deeply affected, sing on.*)

GIRLS

When will the angel find her for you and bring you together? [5]
Who has the love that's stronger than death and faithful forever?

Ach! Wo weilt sie, die dir Gottes Engel einst könne zeigen?
Wo triffst du sie, die bis in den Tod dein bliebe treueigen?

SENTA
(*jumping up, suddenly inspired*)

I do, and I shall be the one to save you! [12]
Angel of God bring us together!
Through me you shall be saved!

Ich sei's, die dich durch ihre Treu' erlöse!
Mög' Gottes Engel mich dir zeigen!
Durch mich sollst du das Heil erreichen!

MARY AND GIRLS
(*jumping up, astonished*)

God help us! Senta! Senta!

Hilf, Himmel! Senta! Senta!

ERIK
(*who has come through the door and overheard Senta's declaration*)

Senta! Would you destroy me?

Senta! Willst du mich verderben?

GIRLS

Help, Erik, help! She's lost her senses!

Helft, Erik, uns! Sie ist von Sinnen!

MARY

My blood runs cold to hear this madness!
I swear I'll have that picture burned
as soon as the master has returned!

Ich fühl' in mir das Blut gerinnen!
Abscheulich Bild, du sollst hinaus,
kommt nur der Vater erst nach Haus!

ERIK
(*gravely*)

Your father's here.

Der Vater kommt.

SENTA
(*suddenly waking out of the mood in which she had remained since the end of the Ballad*)

My father's here?

Der Vater kommt?

ERIK

I saw his ship approach the bay.

Vom Fels sah ich sein Schiff sich nah'n.

MARY

(bustling around)

What did I tell you? He'll appear
and see just how we waste the day!

Nun seht, zu was eu'r Treiben frommt!
Im Hause ist noch nichts gethan.

GIRLS

(joyfully)

They have come home! Let's go and see!

Sie sind daheim! Auf, eilt hinaus!

MARY

(calling the girls together)

Stop! Stop! You'll stay inside with me!
Just think of all your hungry sailors.
So heat the stove without delay!

Halt! Halt! Ihr bleibet fein im Haus!
[28] Das Schiffsvolk kommt mit leerem Magen;
in Küch' und Keller! Säumet nicht!

GIRLS

I wonder what they'll have to tell us!
There's just so much I want to say!

Ach! Wie viel hab' ich ihn zu fragen!
Ich halt mich vor Neugier nicht. —

MARY

Let duty make you doubly zealous, —
You're needed here, so here you stay!

Lasst von der Neugier euch nur plagen, —
vor Allem geht an eure Pflicht!

GIRLS

All right! As soon as dinner's ready,
we've done our duty for today.

Schon gut! Sobald nur aufgetragen,
hält hier uns länger keine Pflicht.

Mary drives the girls out and follows them. / No. 5 Duet / Senta also wants to leave but Erik restrains her.

ERIK

Wait Senta! Can't I have one word with you!
You can reassure my doubts and fears,
or destroy me, ah! if that is what you want!

Bleib', Senta! Bleib' nur einen Augenblick!
Aus meinen Qualen reisse mich! Doch, willst du,
ach, so verdirb mich ganz!

SENTA

(uncertainly)

What doubts? What fears?

Was ist . . .? Was soll?

ERIK

Oh Senta, what will become of me?
Your father's here. Before he leaves again
he must have settled . . . Yes, he must have found you . . .

O, Senta, sprich, was aus mir werden soll?
Dein Vater kommt: eh' wieder er verreis't,
wird er vollbringen, was schon oft er wollte . . .

SENTA

What do you mean?

Und was meinst du?

ERIK

(reaching a desperate conclusion)

Found you a man to marry! — —
I have my faithful love to offer,
my few possessions, my huntsman's skill. —
But when I go to ask your father
he will refuse, I know he will.
Then when this blow will break my heart,
oh Senta, who will take my part?

Dir einen Gatten geben! — —
[29] Mein Herz, voll Treue bis zum Sterben,
mein dürftig Gut, mein Jägerglück: —
darf so um deine Hand ich werben?
Stösst mich dein Vater nicht zurück? —
Wenn sich mein Herz in Jammer bricht, —
sag', Senta, wer dann dür mich spricht?

SENTA

(raising her eyes to him sympathetically, and then turning away)

Ah, Erik, say no more! Please let me go, my father will expect it!
If I'm not there to greet him as he lands,
you know he'd feel neglected.

O, schweige, Erik, jetzt! Lass' mich hinaus, den Vater zu begrüssen!
Wenn nicht, wie sonnst, an Bord die Tochter kommt,
wird er nicht zürnen müssen?

ERIK	
You want to leave me?	Du willst mich flieh'n?
SENTA	
Down to the quay.	Ich muss zum Bord.
ERIK	
Without a word?	Du weichst mir aus!
SENTA	
Do let me be!	Ach, lass mich fort!
ERIK	
You surely know you've hurt my feelings, wounded my faithful love for you? I only ask you for one word of healing, can you not tell me what you'll do? When such despair will break my heart, will Senta speak and take my part?	[29] Fliehst du zurück vor dieser Wunde, die du mir schlugst, im Liebeswahn? O, höre mich zu dieser Stunde, hör' meine letzte Frage an: — wenn dieses Herz in Jammer bricht, wird's Senta sein, die für mich spricht?
SENTA	
What? Was I ever so hard-hearted? You can't believe I'm that unkind? — Oh tell me how such fears were started, what sowed suspicion in your mind?	Wie? Zweifelst du an meinem Herzen? Du zweifelst, ob ich gut dir bin? — Doch sag', was weckt dir solche Schmerzen? Was trübt mit Argwohn deinen Sinn?
ERIK	
Your father, ah, he only thinks of money . . . And Senta, you! How can I really trust you? Have you ever fulfilled one of my wishes? Day after day you break my heart!	Dein Vater, ach! Nach Schätzen geizt er nur . . . Und Senta, du! Wie dürft' auf dich ich zählen? Erfülltest du mir eine meiner Bitten? Kränkst du mein Herz nicht jeden Tag?
SENTA	
Your heart?	Dein Herz?
ERIK	
What should I think, then of the picture?	Was soll ich denken? — Jenes Bild . . .
SENTA	
The picture?	Das Bild?
ERIK	
This infatuation will have to stop!	Lässt du von deiner Schwärmerei wohl ab?
SENTA	
How can I help my eyes from showing pity?	Kann meinem Blick Teilnahme ich verwehren?
ERIK	
Him and his ballad — always on your mind!	Und die Ballade, — heut' noch sangst du sie!
SENTA	
I am a child, I don't know what I'm singing! Now look, really! Are you afraid of a song or a picture?	Ich bin ein Kind, und weiss nicht, was ich singe! O, sag', wie? Fürchtest du ein Lied, ein Bild?
ERIK	
You are so pale . . . Look, should I not be anxious?	Du bist so bleich . . . sag', sollte ich's nicht fürchten?

SENTA

Could such a tragic destiny not move me?

Soll mich des Ärmsten Schreckenslos nicht rühren?

ERIK

I suffer Senta, but you do not care.

Mein Leiden, Senta, rührt es dich nicht mehr?

SENTA

Oh foolish talk! What can your sufferings be?
Are you aware of what his suffering is?

O, prahle nicht! Was kann dein Leiden sein?
Kennst jenes Unglücksel'gen Schicksal du?

(Senta leads Erik close to the picture to explain her meaning.)

Pain and remorse, that's what I see
each time I meet that haunting stare.
Ah, how the force of that cruel decree
can stab my heart with cold despair.

Fühlst du den Schmerz, den tiefen Gram,
mit dem heraub auf mich er sieht?
Ach, was die Ruhe' für ewig ihm nahm,
wie schneidend Weh' durch's Herz mir zieht!

ERIK

Oh no! Now I understand what I dreamt.
God protect you! Satan has trapped your soul!

Weh' mir! Es mahnt mich mein unsel'ger Traum!
Gott schütze dich! Satan hat dich umgarnt!

[30]

SENTA

Now what's wrong with you?

Was er schreckt dich so?

ERIK

Senta, trust me this once!
I dreamt this! Listen and be warned!

Senta! Lass' dir vertrau'n: —
ein Traum ist's! Hör ihn zur Warnung an!

(Senta sits exhausted in the armchair. When Erik begins his story she appears to fall into a magnetic trance so that she actually dreams the dream that Erik relates to her. He stands by the chair.)

ERIK
(in a low voice)

Upon the cliff I lie there dreaming,
watching below the heaving waves.
I hear the seabirds wildly screaming,
the breakers thunder in the caves.
An unknown vessel rides at anchor.
It seems unusual — out of place. [1]
Two seamen row towards the harbour
and one is your father, I know his face.

Auf hohem Felsen lag ich träumend,
sah unter mir des Meeres Flut;
Die Brandung hört' ich, wie sich schäumend
am Ufer brach der Wogen Wut: —
Ein fremdes Schiff am nahen Strande
erblickt' ich, seltsam, wunderbar: —
zwei Männer nahten sich dem Lande,
der ein', ich sah's, dein Vater war.

SENTA
(with closed eyes)

The other?

Der and're?

ERIK

Well I know the man . . .
all dressed in black, and pale and wan . . .

Wohl erkann't ich ihn;
mit schwarzem Wams, die bleiche Mien' . . .

SENTA
(as before)

That haunting stare . . .

Der düst're Blick . . .

ERIK
(indicating the picture)

Yes, it is he!

Der Seemann, er!

SENTA

And I?

Und ich?

ERIK

Run down towards the sea, so glad to see your father out of danger. But scarcely have you rushed to meet him, when suddenly you kneel before the stranger. With passion and with love you greet him . . .	[1]	Du kamst vom Hause her, — du flogst den Vater zu begrüssen; doch kaum noch sah ich an dich langen, du stürztest zu des Fremden Füssen, — ich sah dich seine Knie umfangen . . .

SENTA
(*with increasing excitement*)

I'm in his arms . . .		Er hub mich auf . . .

ERIK

You are on fire, with rapture clinging to his side; you kiss him, mad with wild desire. —		An seine Brust; voll Inbrunst hingst du dich an ihn, — du küsstest ihn mit heisser Lust. —

SENTA

And then?		Und dann?

ERIK
(*watching her with uneasy amazement*)

I see you sail upon the tide.		Sah ich auf's Meer euch flieh'n.

SENTA
(*rapidly awakening and with the greatest enthusiasm*)

He seeks me out! I must be his! I'll go with him to the abyss!	[5]	Er sucht mich auf! Ich muss ihn seh'n! Mit ihm muss ich zu Grunde geh'n!

ERIK

Oh Senta! What will you do! You will be lost! My dream was true!		Entsetzlich! Mir wird es klar! Sie ist dahin! Mein Traum sprach wahr!

Erik rushes out desperate and horrified. After her passionate outburst, Senta falls back into contemplation of the picture. [1] / *No. 6 Finale: Aria, Duet and Trio*

SENTA
(*lightly, but very intensely*)

Ah, wretched man, if you could only find her! May God in Heaven grant you a wife faithful and . . .	[5b]	Ach! möchtest du, bleicher Seemann, sie finden? Betet zum Himmel, dass bald ein Weib Treue ihm . . .

*The door opens and the Dutchman and Daland appear. The Dutchman enters at this moment. Senta's gaze turns from the picture to him and she gives a violent cry of surprise, after which she remains transfixed without taking her eyes off him. Daland waits at the door expecting Senta to come to him.**

SENTA

Ha!		Ha!

(*During the pause the Dutchman remains at the door. He walks slowly forward, his eyes fixed on Senta, and stops.*) [31]

DALAND
(*gradually approaching Senta*)

My child, your father waits to greet you . . . What? No embrace? Not a kiss? You stand there staring like a statue . . . What have I done to merit this?		Mein Kind, du siehst mich auf der Schwelle . . .. Wie? Kein Umarmen? Keinen Kuss? Du bleibst gebannt an deiner Stelle . . . Verdien' ich, Senta, solchen Gruss?

* Wagner's detailed description of the following scene may be found on page 37.

SENTA

(*As Daland reaches her, she grasps his hand.*)

God be with you!	Gott dir zum Gruss!

(*pulling him closer to her*)

I have to know. Who is the stranger?	Mein Vater, sprich! Wer ist der Fremde?

DALAND

(*smiling*)

Don't rush me so!	Drängst du mich?

Aria

Senta, my child, please make this stranger warmly welcome! [32]	Mögst du, mein Kind, den Fremden Mann willkommen heissen!
He is a sailor too, and so an honoured guest.	Seemann ist er, gleich mir; das Gastrecht spricht er an.
Homeless he's wandered far and wide across the ocean,	Lang' ohne Heimat, stets auf fernen, weiten Reisen,
in distant foreign lands his fortune was amassed.	in fremden Landen er der Schätze viel gewann.
But now his wandering years have ended,	Aus seinem Vaterland verwiesen,
he seeks a home and he will pay.	für einen Herd er reichlich lohnt:
So Senta, would you be offended	sprich, Senta, wird es dich verdriessen,
if I invited him to stay?	wenn dieser Fremde bei uns wohnt?

(*to the Dutchman*)

Well, did I overpraise her virtue?	Sagt, hab' ich sie zu viel gepriesen?
See for yourself — make up your mind.	Ihr seht sie selbst, ist sie Euch recht?
Now surely I need not continue?	Soll noch von Lob ich überfliessen?
Admit: a glory to her kind!	Gesteht, sie zieret ihr Geschlecht!

(*The Dutchman makes an affirmative gesture. Daland returns to Senta.*)

Senta, my child, please show him friendship and affection!	Mögst du, mein Kind, dem Manne freundlich dich erweisen!
He comes to ask for your most precious gift in life;	Von deinem Herzen auch spricht holde Gab' er an;
give him your hand, your father blesses this connection;	reich' ihm die Hand, denn Bräutigam sollst du ihn heissen;
if you'll agree, tomorrow you shall be his wife.	stimmst du dem Vater bei, ist morgen er dein Mann.

(*He pulls out some jewels and shows them to Senta.*)

Look at these jewels, come and admire them!	Sieh' dieses Band, sieh' diese Spangen!
And he has more, finer than those.	Was er besitzt, macht dies gering.
Now dearest child, if you desire them —	Muss, teures Kind, dich's nicht verlangen?
accept what he and I propose. [32]	Dein ist es, wechselst du den Ring.

(*Senta keeps her gaze fixed on the Dutchman, and does not look at Daland. Neither does the Dutchman listen to Daland, but is lost in contemplation of the girl.*) [31]

But no-one speaks . . . They have no use for me.	Doch keines spricht . . .Sollt' ich hier lästig sein?
All right! I'll slip away and let them be.	So ist's! Am besten lass' ich sie allein.

(*to Senta*)

Win him, fulfil my last ambition!	Mögst du den edlen Mann gewinnen;
Child, take the chance, while it is there.	glaub' mir, solch' Glück wird nimmer neu.

(*to the Dutchman*)

Stay here with her! It's your decision; —	Bleibt hier allein! Ich geh' von hinnen; —
trust me, she's true as she is fair. [32]	glaubt mir, wie schön, so ist sie treu!

Exit Daland slowly, curious to see whether they will approach one another. He finally goes out in amazed astonishment. The Dutchman and Senta are alone. They remain transfixed, gazing at one another. / Duet [1]

Super duet

DUTCHMAN

Out of the mists of ages unremembered	Wie aus der Ferne längst vergang'ner Zeiten
her gentle image speaks to me:	spricht dieses Mädchens Bild zu mir:
for in my dreams of yearning long unnumbered,	wie ich's geträumt seit langen Ewigkeiten,
this was the face that I would see. —	vor meinen Augen seh' ich's hier. —
Yes, even I have dared to gaze in longing	Wohl hub auch ich voll Sehnsucht meine Blicke
out of the dark upon a woman's face:	aus tiefer Nacht empor zu einem Weib:
this beating heart, preserved by Satan's cunning,	ein schlagend Herz liess, ach! mir Satans Tücke,
stirs and revives the curse of my disgrace.	dass eingedenk ich meiner Qualen bleib!
This dark desire, this flame within me burning,	Die düst're Glut, die hier ich fühle brennen,
what does it signify? Is love returning?	sollt' ich, Unseliger, sie Liebe nennen?
Ah no, salvation is my only goal:	Ach nein! Die Sehnsucht ist es nach dem Heil:
God grant that she may save my wretched soul!	würd' es durch solchen Engel mir zu Teil!

SENTA

Is this a dream, a wonderful illusion?	Versank ich jetzt in wunderbares Träumen,
What I am seeing . . . is it true?	was ich erblicke, ist's ein Wahn?
My childish years, were they a mere delusion?	Weilt' ich bisher in trügerischen Räumen,
Now will my life begin anew?	brach des Erwachens Tag heut' an? —
There is that face, that agonised expression,	Er steht vor mir mit leidenvollen Zügen,
how every feature makes his torment clear:	es spricht sein unerhörter Gram zu mir:
could I ignore the voice of deep compassion?	Kann tiefen Mitleids Stimme mich belügen?
As I'd imagined him, he's standing here!	Wie ich ihn oft geseh'n, so steht er hier.
The raging fire I feel within me burning—	Die Schmerzen, die in meinem Busen brennen,
ah, it torments me. What causes this yearning?	ach! dies Verlangen, wie soll ich es nennen?
I know salvation is your dream, your goal,	Wonach mit Sehnsucht es dich treibt—das Heil,
God in your mercy, let me save his soul!	würd' es, du Ärmster, dir durch mich zu Teil!

[5]

DUTCHMAN

(*approaching Senta*) [31]

Surely you feel you must reject me —	Wirst du des Vaters Wahl nicht schelten?
your father's choice? What! You accept me?	Was er versprach, wie? — dürft' es gelten?
(*He takes one or two steps towards Senta.*)	
How could you give your life to me forever?	Du könntest dich für ewig mir ergeben,
Could you agree? Oh, could you answer yes?	Und deine Hand dem Fremdling reichtest du?
Is this the end of years of vain endeavour?	Soll finden ich nach qualenvollem Leben
Will your sweet faith bring long awaited rest?	in deiner Treu' die lang' ersehnte Ruh'?

SENTA

Who you might be, whatever Fate devises,	Wer du auch sei'st, und welches das Verderben,
to spread its grim destruction in your way:	dem grausam dich dein Schicksal konnte weih'n,
whatever pain my future life comprises,	was auch das Los, das ich mir sollt' erwerben:
my father spoke and so I must obey!	gehorsam werd' ich stets dem Vater sein!

DUTCHMAN

(*with greater emotion*)

So swift and sure? My sorrows seem to move you	So unbedingt, wie? Könnte dich durchdringen
as if you knew my suffering before.	für meine Leiden tiefstes Mitgefühl?

SENTA
(softly to herself)

Oh how you've suffered! How I long to soothe you!

O, welche Leiden? Könnt' ich Trost dir bringen!

DUTCHMAN
(He has heard her call with amazement. Enraptured.)

Sweet notes of peace that pierce the dismal roar!
— You are an angel, and your adoration
uplifts me with its sweet caress!
If there is any hope for my salvation,
Almighty God, with her it rests!

[5] Welch holder Klang im nächtigen Gewühl!
— Du bist ein Engel! Eines Engels Liebe
Verworf'ne selbst zu trösten weiss. —
O, wenn Erlösung mir zu hoffen bliebe,
Allewiger, durch diese sei's!

(falling to his knees)

SENTA

If there is any hope for his salvation
Almighty God, with me it rests!

Ach, wenn Erlösung ihm zu hoffen bliebe,
Allewiger, durch mich nur sei's!

DUTCHMAN
(He sinks down, as though annihilated.)

Ah, if you knew what will befall you,
what dreadful fate you'll have to share;
the sacrifice would so appal you,
it would be far too great to bear!
Your youthful spirit would desert you
with loathing at what this would demand,
if you have not the purest virtue
or perfect faith at your command!

[4] Ach, könntest das Geschick du ahnen,
[5] dem dann mit mir du angehörst,
dich würd' es an das Opfer mahnen,
das du mir bringst, wenn Treu' du schwörst!
Es flöhe schaudernd deine Jugend
dem Lose, dem du sie willst weih'n,
nennst du des Weibes schönste Tugend,
nennst heil'ge Treue du nicht dein!

SENTA
(standing over him)

I know a woman's sacred duty;
trust well in that, unhappy man!
Leave unto Fate the right of judgement
over all those who defy its plan!
Love has revealed my true vocation
I feel its power with every breath.
This is my gift, my consecration.
I'm faithful unto death.

[4] Wohl kenn' ich Weibes heil'ge Pflichten,
sei d'rum getrost, unsel'ger Mann!
Lass' über die das Schicksal richten,
die seinem Spruche trotzen kann!
In meines Herzens höchster Reine
kenn' ich der Treue Hochgebot: —
Wem ich sie weih', schenk' ich die Eine:
Die Treue bis zum Tod!

DUTCHMAN
(with solemn emotion and exaltation)

These noble words, this declaration
pour balm upon my wounded soul.
Hear this: at last I find salvation,
Powers who thrust me back to hell!
Star of misfortune, dim your glory!
Light of my hope shine forth anew!
You angel, though you once ignored me,
strengthen this heart and keep it true!

Ein heil'ge Balsam meinen Wunden
dem Schwur, dem hohen Wort entfliesst.
Hört es: mein Heil hab' ich gefunden,
Mächte, die ihr zurück mich stiess't!
Du, Stern des Unheils, sollst erblassen!
Licht meiner Hoffnung, leuchte neu!
Ihr Engel, die mich einst verlassen,
stärkt jetzt dies Herz in seiner Treu!

SENTA

Inspired by wonder and elation
my task is clear, my mission sure.
Here he has found his destination,
here may he rest, his ship secure!
What is this mighty power which assaults me?
What wild emotion binds me to you?
Almighty, may the force that exalts me
strengthen this heart and make it true!

Von mächt'gem Zauber überwunden,
reisst mich's zu seiner Rettung fort:
Hier habe Heimat er gefunden,
hier ruh' sein Schiff in sichrem Port!
[33] Was ist's, das mächtig in mir lebet?
Was schliesst berauscht mein Busen ein?
Allmächt'ger, was mich hoch erhebet,
lass' es die Kraft der Treue sein!

(Re-enter Daland who remains at a suitable distance. Trio) [34]

DALAND

Forgive me! I can't restrain my thirsty crew.	Verzeiht! Mein Volk hält draussen sich nicht mehr,
We give a party when the ship comes home.	nach jeder Rückkunft, wisset, giebt's ein Fest:
Now what an occasion, though it's up to you,	Verschönern möcht' ich's, komme deshalb her,
if your engagement also were made known.	ob mit Verlobung sich's vereinen lässt? —
I think your courtship was a fine success.	Ich denk', ihr habt nach Herzenswunsch gefreit?
Senta, my child, say, will you answer "yes"?	Senta, mein Kind, sag', bist du auch bereit?

SENTA
(with solemn resolution)

Here is my hand, here is my heart,	Hier meine Hand! Und ohne Reu'
and unto death we shall not part!	bis in den Tod gelob' ich Treu'!

DUTCHMAN

She gives her hand, her faithful heart	Sie reicht die Hand! Gesprochen sei
curbs Satan's will and mocks his art!	Hohn, Hölle, dir durch ihre Treu'!

DALAND

This match rejoices every heart!	Euch soll dies Bündnis nicht gereu'n!
Be glad! Let celebrations start!	Zum Fest! Heut' soll sich alles freu'n!

The curtain falls. [33]

Daland (Dennis Wicks) tells Senta (Josephine Barstow) that they have a guest in the 1982 ENO production by David Pountney. (photo: Reg Wilson)

Act Three

A bay with rocky shores. In the foreground, to one side, is Daland's house; in the background, near together, the two ships, 'Norwegian' and 'Dutchman'. It is a clear night. The Norwegian ship is lit up, and the sailors are on deck, feasting and singing. The Dutchman's ship presents a strange contrast; an unnatural darkness broods over it, and a deathlike silence reigns. [17, 14, 11] / *No. 7 Scene and Chorus*

CHORUS OF NORWEGIAN SAILORS

Steersman leave the watch! [11]
Steersman come to us!
Ho! He! Ye! Ha! [14]
Let the anchor go! Furl the sail!
Steersman here!
Do we care what reef and storm can do?
No, tonight the wind can blow its worst!
When you know your girl is bringing you baccy for your pipe and brandy for your thirst!
Hussassahe!
Tempest and storm—
Yollohohe!
Laugh them to scorn!

Steuermann, lass' die Wacht!
Steuermann, her zu uns!
Ho! He! Je! Ha!
Hisst die Segel auf! Anker fest!
Steuermann, her!
Fürchten weder Wind, noch bösen Strand,
wollen heute 'mal recht lustig sein!
Jeder hat sein Mädel auf dem Land,
herrlichen Tabak und guten Branntewein.
Hussassahe!
Klipp' und Sturm draus —
Jollohohe!
Lachen wir aus!

(*They dance on the deck marking each measure with loud stamps of their feet. The girls come out of the house carrying baskets of food and drink.*) [17]

GIRLS

My, look at them! What dainty feet! [35]
So skilful, no woman could compete!

Mein! Seht doch an! Sie tanzen gar!
Der Mädchen bedarf's da nicht fürwahr.

(*They go towards the Dutchman's ship.*)

SAILORS

Women! Stop! Come over here!

He! Mädel! Halt! Wo geht ihr hin?

GIRLS

Your longing for your wine and beer?
Well you must wait, your neighbours need them.
And as the guests they should come first.

Steht euch nach frischem Wein der Sinn?
Eu'r Nachbar dort soll auch 'was haben,
ist Trank und Schmaus für euch allein?

STEERSMAN

You're right! Go on, you go and feed them,
or else I think they'll die of thirst.

Fürwahr! Tragt's hin den armen Knaben!
Vor Durst sie scheinen matt zu sein.

SAILORS

How still they seem!

Man hört sie nicht!

STEERSMAN

And silent too!
No lights, not an inkling of the crew!

Ei! seht doch nur!
Kein Licht! Von der Mannschaft keine Spur!

GIRLS

(*From the shore, calling to the Dutchman's ship*)

Hey, shall we bring a light for you? —
Where have you gone? What's wrong with you?

He! Seeleut'! He! Wollt Fackeln ihr? —
Wo seid ihr doch? Man sieht nicht hier!

SAILORS

Ha ha ha!
Still fast asleep, they're dreaming on!

Ha ha ha!
Weckt sie nicht auf! Sie schlafen noch!

GIRLS

He! Sailors! He! Where have you gone?	He! Seeleut'! He! Antwortet doch!

(*a long silence*) [36]

SAILORS
(*mocking, with affected sorrow*)

Haha! Poor creatures, they are dead! They drink no wine and eat no bread!	Haha! Wahrhaftig! Sie sind tot; sie haben Speis' und Trank nicht not!

GIRLS

You sailors, you cannot just lie there in bed!	Ei, Seeleute? Liegt ihr so faul schon im Nest?
Get up and enjoy the dancing instead!	Ist heute für euch denn nicht auch ein Fest?

SAILORS

They lie in deepest sleep on board, like Fafner with his golden hoard!	Sie liegen fest auf ihrem Platz, wie Drachen hüten sie den Schatz!

GIRLS

Our wine is so cool, our bread fresh and warm,	He, Seeleute! Wollt ihr nicht frischen Wein?
surely you're thirsty after the storm?	Ihr müsset wahrlich doch durstig auch sein!

SAILORS

They neither sing nor drink at all, and round their ship the darkness falls.	Sie trinken nicht, sie singen nicht; in ihrem Schiffe brennt kein Licht.

GIRLS

Well, if you've no girl friends on land any more,	Sagt! Habt ihr denn nicht auch ein Schätzchen am Land?
Why not come and dance with us here on the shore?	Wollt ihr nicht mit tanzen auf grünem Strand?

SAILORS

So weak and wasted, pale and wan, and all their sweethearts dead and gone!	Sie sind schon alt und bleich, statt rot, — und ihre Liebsten, die sind tot!

GIRLS
(*calling ever louder and more anxiously*)

You sailors! Sailors are you there? There's plenty of meat and drink to spare!	He! Seeleut'! Seeleut'! Wacht doch auf! Wir bringen euch Speise and Trank zu Hauf!

(*A long silence.* [36] *The girls are taken aback and fearful.*)

Yes, really, yes, they must be dead! They drink no wine and eat no bread.	Wahrhaftig, ja! Sie scheinen tot! Sie haben Speis' und Trank nicht not.

SAILORS
(*with increasing high spirits*)

You've heard of the Flying Dutchman's fate!	Vom fliegenden Holländer wisst ihr ja!
Well, there is his ship, just as legend relates!	Sein Schiff, wie es leibt, wie es lebt, seht ihr da!

GIRLS

This crew will slumber many a year, they are not men, but ghosts, we fear!	So weckt die mannschaft ja nicht auf! Gespenster sind's, wir schwören d'rauf!

SAILORS

For hundreds of years have you sailed on the seas,	Wie viel hundert Jahr seid ihr zur See?
undamaged by shipwreck, untouched by disease!	Euch thut ja der Sturm und die Klippe nicht weh!

GIRLS

They neither sing nor drink at all, and round their ship the darkness falls.	Sie trinken nicht! Sie singen nicht! In ihrem Schiffe brennt kein Licht.

SAILORS

And have you no letters, no business to do?	Habt ihr keine Brief', keine Aufträg' für's Land?
For our great great grandfather's waiting for you!	Unsern Urgrossvätern wir bringen zur Hand!

GIRLS

So weak and wasted, pale and wan, and all their sweethearts dead and gone!	Sie sind schon alt, und bleich statt rot! und ihre Liebsten, ach! sind tot!

SAILORS
(noisily)

Let's see how you sail her, let's see what you know.	Hei! Seeleute! Spannt eure Segel doch auf,
Let's see just how swiftly the 'Dutchman' can go!	und zeigt uns des fliegenden Holländers Lauf!

GIRLS
(moving fearfully away from the Dutchman's ship)

Just look at it, we dread it here! What use to call — they cannot hear!	Sie hören nicht! Uns graus't es hier! Sie wollen nichts, — was rufen wir?

SAILORS

Just leave them, they are dead and gone! But for the living, life goes on!	Ihr Mädel, lasst die Toten ruh'n! Lasst's uns Lebend'gen gütlich thun!

GIRLS
(handing their baskets to the sailors over the side of the ship)

Since they don't want it, it is yours!	So nehmt: der Nachbar hat's verschmäht.

STEERSMAN AND SAILORS

What? Don't you want to stay with us?	Wie? Kommt ihr denn nicht selbst an Bord?

GIRLS

No, not just now, there's plenty of time! We shall come back, you drink the wine, and with your dainty dancing feet mind that you let your neighbours sleep!	Ei, jetzt noch nicht! Es ist ja nicht spät! Wir kommen bald, jetzt trinkt nur fort, und, wenn ihr wollt, so tanzt dazu, nur gönnt dem müden Nachbar Ruh!

Exeunt Girls.

SAILORS
(emptying the baskets)

Hurrah! Hurrah! Here's food in plenty! Let's thank that sleepy crew!	Juchhe! Juchhe! Da giebt's die Fülle! — Liebe Nachbar', habe Dank!

STEERSMAN

Drink up, till every flask is empty! Good neighbours this is thanks to you!	Zum Rand sein Glas ein jeder fülle! Lieb Nachbar liefert uns den Trank.

SAILORS

Wake up, if you can find your voice,	Lieb' Nachbar'n habt ihr Stimm' und Sprach',
then join with us and let's rejoice! [37]	so wachet auf und macht's uns nach!

(From now on, there is movement on the Dutchman's ship. The Norwegian sailors continue laughing, drinking up and clanking their mugs.)

Steersman, leave the watch! [11]	Steuermann, lass' die Wacht!
Steersman, come to us!	Steuermann, her zu uns!
Ho! He! Ye! Ha! [14]	Ho! He! Je! Ha!
Let the anchor go! Furl the sail!	Hisst die Segel auf! Anker fest!
Steersman here!	Steuermann, her! —

We have kept the watch by wind and rain,
forced to drink the ocean's filthy brine.
Now we'll fill our bellies full again,
now the girls have brought their finest brandy wine.
Tempest and storm! Yollolohe!
Laugh them to scorn! Hussassahe!
Hussassahe! Steersman come!
Drink with us! [17]

Wachten manche Nacht in Sturm und Graus,
tranken oft des Meer's gesalz'nes Nass:
heute wachen wir bei Saus und Schmaus,
besseres Getränk giebt Mädel uns vom Fass.
Klipp und Sturm drauss, Jollolohe!
Lachen wir aus! Hussassahe!
Hussassahe! Steuermann her!
Trink mit uns!

The sea, whilst remaining calm everywhere else, begins to seethe around the Dutchman's ship; a dark blue flame flares up as a watch fire. A fierce storm wind blows through the rigging. The crew, who had previously been unseen, seem to be raised to life by the light of the flame.

CREW OF THE 'DUTCHMAN'

Yohohe! Yohohe! Hoe! Hoe! Hoe! [1, 14]
Huissa! [15]
To the land drives the storm — [2]
Huissa!
Reef the sail! Make her fast!
Huissa!
Bring her into the bay! — [30]
Haunted captain, go on land,
seven years have passed away!
Seek the golden maiden's hand!
Seek the love that won't betray!
Happy day! Hui!
Marry her! Hui!
Gales blow a tune for him. —
Waves do a dance for him!
Hui! — Did he call? [15]
— Is he there? Has he returned?
Hui! — Hoist the sail! —
But the bride, where can she be?
Hui! — To the sea!
Without aim! Without hope! Have you failed once again?
Hahaha!
Howling wind and storm make moan,
hurl at us the rising sea.
Satan guards us as his own,
safe in all eternity.

Johohe! Johohe! Hoe! Hoe! Hoe!
Huissa!
Nach dem Land treibt der Sturm —
Huissa!
Segel ein! Anker los!
Huissa!
In die Bucht laufet ein! —
Schwarzer Hauptmann, geh' an's Land,
sieben Jahre sind vorbei!
Frei' um blonden Mädchens Hand!
Blondes Mädchen, sei ihm treu!
Lustig heut'! Hui!
Bräutigam! Hui!
Sturmwind heult Brautmusik, —
Ozean tanzt dazu!
Hui! — Horch, er pfeift: —
— Kapitän, bist wieder da? —
Hui! — Segel auf! —
Deine Braut, sag', wo sie blieb?
— Hui! — Auf in See!
Kapitän! Kapitän! Hast kein Glück in der Lieb!
Hahaha!
Sause, Sturmwind, heule zu!
Uns'ren Segeln lässt du Ruh'!
Satan hat sie uns gefeit,
reissen nicht in Ewigkeit.

The Norwegian crew have listened, first with amazement, then with horror. During the Dutch crew's song, their ship is tossed to and fro on raging waves, a furious gale howls and whistles through the bare rigging. / Elsewhere, the sky and sea remain as calm as before.

NORWEGIAN SAILORS

What a song! — Are they ghosts? —
I'm afraid! — We must sing —
Sing our song! — Sing it loud! —
Steersman leave the watch! (*etc.*) [11]

Welcher Sang? — Ist es Spuk? —
Wie mich's graut! — Stimmet an! —
Unser Lied! — Singet laut! —
Steuermann, lass' die Wacht! (*etc.*)

CREW OF THE 'DUTCHMAN'

Howling wind and storm make moan [1, 2]
(*etc.*)

Sause, Sturmwind, heule zu!
(*etc.*)

The Norwegian sailors are silenced by the storm and the ever louder and wilder song of the ghostly crew. They leave their deck, terrified, making the sign of the cross, which is greeted with loud laughs of scorn: — the deathly stillness returns to the Dutchman's ship immediately, and it is shrouded in darkness. The sky and sea become calm again. [36] */ No. 8 Finale / Senta hurries out of the house, followed by Erik, who is greatly agitated. / Duet*

ERIK

What are you saying? God, what can you mean?
It's madness! Really? Is it true?

Was musst' ich hören! Gott, was musst' ich sehen!
Ist's Täuschung? Wahrheit? Ist es That?

SENTA

No, do not ask. I cannot answer or explain it.

[38] O, frage nicht! Antwort darf ich nicht geben.

ERIK

Almighty God! You mean it! It is true!
What evil has ensnared you in its power?
What kind of force beguiled you so?
What kind of force has urged you on so fas
On to destroy this faithful, loving heart!
Your father, ah, this bridegroom came here with him . . .
I think I know what passed between those two.
But you . . . how can you? —
How can you accept a man
who you have never seen before?

Gerechter gott! Kein Zweifel! Es ist wahr!
Welch' unheilvolle Macht riss dich dahin?
Welche Gewalt verführte dich?
[39] Welche Gewalt verführte dich so schnell?
Grausam zu brechen dieses treustes Herz?
Dein Vater, ha! — den Bräut'gam bracht' er mit . . .
wohl kenn' ich ihn, mir ahnte, was geschieht!
Doch du . . . ist's möglich! —
Reichest deine hand dem Mann,
der deine Schwelle kaum betrat?

SENTA
(in a turmoil)

Don't ask me! No! I must! I must!

Nicht weiter! Schweig! Ich muss, ich muss!

ERIK

Oh such obedience! Blind just like the deed!
You welcome the slightest suggestion from your father;
a single blow and I do not exist!

[39] O des Gehorsams, blind wie deine That!
Den Wink des Vaters nanntest du willkommen,
mit einem Stoss vernichtest due mein Herz!

SENTA

No more! No more! I must not see you again,
nor even think of you: sacred duty commands it.

Nicht mehr! Nicht mehr! Ich darf dich nicht mehr seh'n,
nicht an dich denken: — hohe Pflicht gebeut's.

ERIK

Which sacred duty? — You gave an oath to me —
of love everlasting; that was not sacred?

Welch' hohe Pflicht? Ist's höh're nicht, zu halten,
Was du mir einst gelobtest, ewige Treue?

SENTA
(greatly shocked)

What? Did I promise everlasting love?

Wie? Ew'ge Treue hätt' ich dir gelobt?

ERIK
(in agony)

Senta, oh Senta, could you deny it?

Senta, O Senta, leugnest du?

Cavatina

Can't you recall that clear midsummer morning?
You called to me, we walked upon the hill.
I gathered flowers. Heedless of your warning,
love gave me strength to reach them higher still.
I lay beside you, the cliff swept down before us,
we watched your father's ship put out to sea.
That very morning, your father, when he saw us,
had, to my joy, entrusted you to me.
So when you clasped me tight in your embrace,
then surely you affirmed your love once more?

[40] Willst jenes Tags du nicht dich mehr entsinnen,
als du vom Fels mich riefest in das Thal?
Als, dir des Hochlands Blume zu gewinnen,
mutvoll ich trug Beschwerden ohne Zahl?
Gedenkst du, wie auf steilem Felsenriffe
vom Ufer wir den Vater scheiden sah'n?
Er zog dahin auf weiss beschwingtem Schiffe,
und meinem Schutz vertraute er dich an: —
als sich dein Arm um meinen Nacken schlang,
gestandest Liebe du mir nicht auf's neu'?

And when your eyes were gazing at my face —
did I imagine the oath of love they swore?

Was bei der Hände Druck mich hehr durchdrang —
sag', war's nicht die Versich'rung deiner Treu'?

The Dutchman has overheard the previous scene and now rushes forward in wild and terrifying excitement.

DUTCHMAN

Betrayal! My salvation!
Lost till the end of time!

Verloren! Ach verloren!
Ewig verlor'nes Heil!

ERIK
(*stepping back, dismayed*)

What is this? God!

Was seh' ich? Gott!

DUTCHMAN

Senta, farewell!

Senta, leb' wohl!

SENTA
(*barring his way*)

No wait! Poor creature!

Halt ein, Unsel'ger!

ERIK
(*to Senta*)

You must leave him!

Was beginnst du?

DUTCHMAN

To sea! Away to sea forever! —
(*to Senta*)
For you have broken your faith,
and my salvation is destroyed!
Farewell! I never could destroy you.

In See! In See! — Für ew'ge Zeiten! —
Um deine Treue ist's gethan, —
um deine Treue, — um mein Heil!
Leb' wohl, ich will dich nicht verderben!

ERIK

He's a madman! Come away!

Entsetzlich! Dieser Blick . . .!

SENTA
(*to the Dutchman*)

No wait!
I swear I shall not let you go!

Halt ein!
Von dannen sollst du nimmer flieh'n!

DUTCHMAN
(*He gives a shrill blast on his whistle* [15] *and shouts to his crew:*)

Cast her off! Put to sea! [2, 3]
Say your farewell, farewell to land forever!

Segel auf! Anker los!
Sagt Lebewohl auf Ewigkeit dem Lande!

Trio

SENTA

You doubt my word, you do not trust me? [38]
How could you ever be so blind?
Stay here! I keep what I have promised!
No power on earth can change my mind!

Ha! Zweifelst du an meiner Treue?
Unsel'ger, was verblendet dich?
Halt ein! Das Bündnis nicht bereue!
Was ich gelobte, halte ich!

ERIK

What is this? God! Can I believe it?
Can I believe what I am forced to see?
Senta! You are in Satan's power.
Come here, for I would set you free!

Was hör' ich! Gott, was muss ich sehen?
Muss ich dem Ohr, dem Auge trau'n?
Senta! Willst du zu Grunde gehen?
Zu mir! Du bist in Satan's Klau'n!

DUTCHMAN

Once more the sea waits to receive me!
Both you and God betray my trust!
Your oaths of love only deceive me,
all that you promised was a jest!

Fort auf das Meer treibt's mich auf' neue!
Ich zweifl' an dir, ich zweifl' an Gott!
Dahin! Dahin ist alle Treue!
Was du gelobtest, war dir Spott!

Now learn the dreadful fate from which you have been saved!	Erfahre das Geschick, vor dem ich dich bewahr!
For I am condemned to such terrible perdition,	Verdammt bin ich zum grässlichsten der Lose:
death were to me a joy beyond belief!	zehnfacher Tod wär' mir erwünschte Lust!
I could be saved, but only by a woman	Vom Fluch ein Weib allein kann mich erlösen,
whose love was constant in the face of death.	ein Weib, das Treu' bis in den Tod mir hält.
You did indeed declare your love . . . but only	Wohl hast du Treue mir gelobt . . . doch vor
to me and not to God. That saved your soul!	dem Ewigen noch nicht: — Dies rettet dich!
Then know the dreaful fate that lies in store	Denn wiss', Unsel'ge, welches das Geschick,
for those whose sacred vows to me are broken:	das jene trifft, die mir die Treue brechen:
Endless damnation is their fate! —	Ew'ge Verdammnis ist ihr Los! —
Countless victims have already paid	Zahllose Opfer fielen diesem Spruch
the price: but Senta, I have saved your soul.	durch mich: — du aber sollst gerettet sein!
Farewell! For I am damned forevermore!	Leb' wohl! — Fahr' hin, mein Heil in Ewigkeit!

ERIK

(*calling in wild anxiety to the house and to the Norwegian ship*)

God help her! Help her! Rescue her!	Zu Hilfe! Rettet! Rettet sie!

SENTA

(*stopping the Dutchman*)

I know you well! Well I know your fate.	Wohl kenn' ich dich! Wohl kenn' ich dein Geschick;
When I saw you I knew that it must be you!	ich kannte dich, als ich zuerst dich sah!
Your quest is at an end! — Yes, it	Das Ende deiner Qual ist da! — Ich bin's,
shall be my love which saves you at the last!	durch deren Treu' dein Heil du finden sollst!

ERIK

Oh God! He has bewitched her!	Helft ihr! Sie ist verloren!

(*At Erik's cry for help, Daland, Mary, the girls from the house, and the sailors from the ship, run on.*)

MARY, DALAND, CHORUS

What is happening?	Was erblick' ich!

DUTCHMAN

You cannot know or dream just who I am!	Du kennst mich nicht, du ahnst nicht wer ich bin!

(*He points to his ship, where the blood red sails are now spread, and his spectral crew are busily preparing for departure.*)

But every sea and every ocean, and every	Befrag' die Meere aller Zonen, frag'
sailor who sails across the world	den Seemann, der den Ozean durchstrich: —
will know this ship, the terror of the godly:	er kennt dies Schiff, das Schrecken aller Frommen:
the "Flying Dutchman" is my name!	den "fliegenden Holländer" nennt man mich!

(*The Dutchman, with the speed of lightning, boards his ship, which instantly heads out to sea. Senta tries to follow him but is held back by Daland, Erik and Mary.*)

CREW OF THE "DUTCHMAN"

Yohohoe! Yohohoe! Hoyohoe! Hoe! [1, 14]	Johohoe! Johohoe! Hojohoe! Hoe!

MARY, DALAND, ERIK, CHORUS

Senta! Senta! What does this mean?	Senta! Senta! — Was willst du thun?

(*Senta frees herself with the strength of anger from their grasp and runs to the edge of the cliff overhanging the sea, whence she calls with all her might, to the Dutchman, who is sailing away.*)

SENTA

Praised be that angel and her decree!	Preis' deinen Engel und sein Gebot!
Since I am faithful, you are free!	Hier steh' ich, treu dir bis zum Tod!

(*She throws herself into the sea. Immediately the Dutchman's ship sinks with all hands into the waves. The sea heaves and falls in a whirlpool. In the red glow of the rising sun, Senta and the Dutchman, transfigured, are seen, in a close embrace, rising from the wreck of the vessel, and soaring upwards.*) [5, 12, 1]

Curtain.

Josef Svoboda's design for Act One (the appearance of the Dutchman's ship) at Bayreuth. (Festspielleitung Bayreuth)

Discography Available recordings in stereo (unless asterisked *) and in German. Cassette tape numbers are also given. A valuable review by William Mann of all performances on record is contained in *Opera on Record* (ed. Alan Blyth, Hutchinson 1979).

Conductor **Company/ Orchestra**	*Keilberth* **Bayreuth Festival**	*Dorati* **Royal Opera Covent Garden**	*Böhm* **Bayreuth Festival**	*Solti* **Chicago SO**	*Konwitschny* **Berlin State Opera**
Dutchman	Uhde	London	Stewart	Bailey	Fischer-Dieskau
Senta	Varnay	Rysanek	Jones	Martin	Schech
Daland	Weber	Tozzi	Ridderbusch	Talvela	Frick
Erik	Lustig	Liebl	Esser	Kollo	Schock
Steersman	Traxel	Lewis	Ek	Krenn	Wunderlich
Mary	Schärtel	Elias	Wagner	I. Jones	Wagner
Disc number UK	**D97D3**	**2BB109–11**	**2720052**	**D24D3**	**SLS 5226**
Disc number USA	**SRS 63519**	**OSA1399**	**2709040**	**OSA13119**	**S–3616**
Tape number			**3371017**	**K24K32**	**TC SLS 5226**
Excerpts		**SDD439**		**SET626**	
Excerpts (tape)				**KCET626**	

Excerpts

	Artists	Disc Number	Tape Number
Overture	VPO cond. Knappertsbusch	ECS672	
Overture	Philharmonia cond. Klemperer	SXLP30436	TC–SXLP30436
Overture	Berlin PO cond. Karajan	ASD3160	
Overture	Cleveland cond. Szell	61623	
Overture	New Philharmonia cond. Paita	LOD 770	LOC 770
Overture	Czech PO cond. Konwitschny	114076.0	
Overture	VPO cond. Stein	SXL6656	KSXC6656
Overture	LPO cond. Boult	ASD 3071	
Overture	Philharmonia cond. Karajan	SXLP 30506	TC–SXLP 30506
Overture	LPO cond. Downes	CFP 40287	TC–CFP 40287
Overture	Chicago SO cond. Solti	SXL 6856	KSX 6856
Overture	Dresden Staatskapelle cond. Varviso	6570 030	
Overture	VPO cond. Böhm	2531 288	3301 288
Daland's aria	Greindl	RL30439	
Senta's ballad	Nilsson	6500 294	
Senta's ballad	Sass	SLPX11940	
Senta's ballad	Sutherland	SXL6930	KSXC 6930

Bibliography

Carl Dahlhaus in *Richard Wagner's Music Dramas* (trans. Mary Whittall; Cambridge, 1979) has a very illuminating chapter on the opera.

Apart from chapters in general biographies of the composer, such as those by Ernest Newman (London 1933–47, revised 1976) and Curt von Westernhagen, little has been written about *The Flying Dutchman*, relative to the numerous studies of other aspects of Wagner. Frank Granville-Barker's book on the opera (Barrie and Jenkins, 1979) is the exception and contains lively introductory chapters, especially on the literary antecedents of the story.

Heine's *Memoirs of Herr von Schnabelewopski* is a delightfully amusing section of his *Tableaux de Voyage*, which may be found in editions of his complete prose works.

Wagner's own writings are, of course, worth attention: apart from those reprinted in this book, *A Communication to my Friends*, and his autobiography, *My Life*, are especially relevant. (*Complete Prose Works,* translated by W. Ashton Ellis.)

The anthology, edited and translated by R. Jacobs and G. Skelton, *Wagner Writes from Paris: Stories, Essays, and Articles by the Young Composer* (London, 1973) contains the best of Wagner's journalism during the years of waiting for *Rienzi's* production at the Opéra.